DAY TO NIGHT

DAY TO NIGHT

KIJUAN M. MURPHY

To order additional copies of this book, contact:
Xlibris
844-714-8691
www.Xlibris.com
Orders@Xlibris.com
819511

ACKNOWLEDGEMENT:

MOM

GRANDMOTHER

GRANDFATHER

UNCLE

TO MY FRIENDS

&

TO THE PEOPLE OF QUINCY

CONTENTS

PROLOGUE

The First Beginning

To start this off, I will give you a little run-down of who I am. My name's Kijuan (Ki-Juan), but my friends have been calling me Ki since I got out of the hospital, maybe before then, but I took that name and made it Key. As in the key to happiness, wealth, and soon to be romance. I am also the first black lacrosse player to score a goal for the Quincy High School boys lacrosse team. I don't remember how that felt, but I know that had to be amazing. But basically that shows exactly how dramatic life changes for the first example, considering I don't even remember that moment. I say that because I think you could imagine how good life was going for me for it to just crash like that, literally and figuratively.

Another example will show you how I was with girls---the way things went with them, how easy they came, and how they came. One time I was at my friend's house and we were bored, so we called some girls over to swim in the pool. It was late so someone called the cops and I hid in the bushes. then they ran back into his apartment after I was safe, and we all just went back to the apartment. It was a fun thing to hear about, and that is why I felt the need to jot that time down that my friend reminded me of.

Football was fun; I enjoyed it just as much as lacrosse because I was playing that sport since I was six years old. I was a middle linebacker then, And I played a little defensive end in high school as well. I know I had to have had a few championship trophies, and I saw a two-year varsity letterman with the Panthers at my grandmother's house. In my final year playing for them, I think we won a championship--- us or the Elks. But we were in that game, and I haven't done that since I was six with the Riverdale Buccaneers.

I volunteered in Germantown, which is a town in Quincy where I was a camp counselor at a camp I used to attend as a camper and eventually worked at. That was fun, but I just grew out of it, and it became repetitive. We went on field trips, and as a volunteer, it felt no different from a camper. But when you were getting paid to counsel, it was another story. My sister did end up going there as a camper too. I don't know if she will do the volunteering and working, but that setting molds you well.

After being born and attending Montclair in Quincy, Massachusetts, I moved to Georgia around second grade. I still remember my second-grade teacher's name, Ms. Mcmillion or something along those lines. I'll get into more of Georgia later in the book, but one thing I'll say now and may say again is living in Georgia made me able to conduct myself properly in various settings or even temperatures, considering how dry the heat was in comparison to up north.

Massachusetts came back into the picture around sixth grade, which was when I came back to Quincy, which started off different but then I began to get into school and sports. During the summer, I was in the summer camp I told you I would eventually work at. That was fun; I think I met some lifelong friends there because we still hang out with one another and consider one another close friends.

I had a brother my mother signed me up for with the Big Brothers Association in Georgia, but I guess he changed his number or something because I haven't spoken to him but remember calling him.

Speaking of my "brother," he taught me how to roller-skate. I remember going out with him a lot to roller rinks and doing fun stuff like that. I could never get as good as him, but I was out there and did do my thing. We went to a few places like aquariums, mini amusement parks, One that I sort of remember is dixie funland which is now called the fun spot I believe. He taught me how to be a better man with things like that, when he took me to church specifically, that's where he played the drums and he would tend to let me play. like that. I enjoyed that, I may just end up trying that phone number again tomorrow. Considering he is in Georgia, I won't see him anytime soon, but it would be nice to hear his voice.

I have had a few jobs in my life. I started cutting grass early with an older stepfather of mine. That started in Georgia, and that is good because I don't see anyone lugging lawn mowers around Quincy. It was a nice job; it gave me character and ambition. I say character because I still remember the sweat from the dry heat we were in and knocking on countless amounts of doors to cut their grass. Ambition because I knew that me going through that will end in me being paid; the value of a dollar never changed.

After I moved up here, I got another job around ninth grade. It was hard to implement that with sports, but I had to have made it work because I do not hear anything about it today. I was a waiter at an elderly home, I believe. That didn't last long, but then I was at Party City for a while only to end up at a few stores in the mall. My first job at the mall was Sears, and then I was at a sneaker store but then got into a jersey store, which sold hats too. I may use my plug with Securitas to get me into a store I see has their security in the mall now.

I say Securitas because that is whom I currently work for. I do security for them at TD Garden mostly, but they have had me at a few other spots like a casino and one time had me in a law school. They are a smooth company, but depending on your supervisor, they might not pay you for all your hours, so be careful. Like when I'm at TD Garden, they only pay me for like two hours when I really am there for a slick 5 hours but my supervisor at the casino paid me a little more, so respect to him.

CHAPTER 1

New Beginnings

I really do not know how to start this chapter, but I will start by saying this: I feel like I don't have that many chances left and that could change in a matter of seconds. I really do not know if there is a separation between academic chances, relationship chances, and life in-general chances. I think I said that last time I had a little peek at the trenches, but I think I can do that. Let's hope I can. Something that will be happening is that I will put this behind me because that past does not hold healing, but my future will, This will be hard because everything reminds me of that accident when driving, but I try my best to make amends with thoughts related to that.

I see myself in the future being comfortable wondering, *Why was I so scared?* I'm just hoping that is real life and not imagination. Basically in the book, I will be talking about things that have happened in my life that have molded me into the man Writing this today. That happens to be a lot and worth a story. This story should also give adolescents a way to think when dealing with similar or even any dilemmas because I know people Who just stopped and said things like "I don't know what to think" or "I don't know what to do."

Sometimes you can't depend on people the way you think you can based on how life is going at that time. Life can switch on you at any time instantly. That has happened to me numerous times. I knew it, I said it all the time, and I was living my life as happy as I could be. And it was one thing, if not the other, that ruined all of it, but it is okay, just lessons being learned, if not relearned. It taught me to stay on my toes in every aspect of life. I am sincerely sorry for not doing that; I thought I was. That was just me trying to be cool in a society where it really did not matter.

I was still in my high school state of mind, young-minded. The good half of high school that I remembered, the times I enjoyed with girls, sports, and parties. I really do not remember anything negative about high school; I don't know if it is because I am older so I don't mind homework because I remember it but don't mind it. I believe that is because I spent my freshman year of college in a community college right next to my high school because I had to, so I am not blaming it on that. I eventually was able to figure it out in its worst fashion; I had seen little signs, called them out, but still did not change the way I thought. I thought at least the people you'd meet in college would be trustworthy, but nope.

I'm really dumb. I just wanted things to all look the exact way it was at the time. I tried my hardest. I really do not know why, but I just will not spend the rest of my life looking for an answer—Just take my L in stride. Sometimes I would be like, "Nah, what am I thinking?" But I don't know when I went into the meeting to discuss what happened and the bag that belonged to a former classmate of mine, but I was not present where the bag was discovered, so at first it was, "Stick to the plan." But this is the ridiculous part. Three minutes into that meeting I said "THIS HAD NOTHING TO DO WITH ME!"

I gave her some quick bullshit-ass stories she easily found flaws in, and she wouldn't believe the one true thing that came out of my mouth. The truth really was not setting me free. I mean, I guess if I stuck to the lies, I could respect what I was going through. But I made up my mind too late. Even after the meeting, I wrote her a letter apologizing for my lies because I understood the negatives behind lying but soon realized she really did not care that I lied. She did that because I was black. It was the only reasonable thing that made sense to her. "He's black. Of course, it's his." I never even got the weed or the bag, and I knew they were not about to just toss it out. A ten-minute conversation thought it could ruin twenty years of existence like that because having something like that on your record is not good, so it has to be bad; that's why I said that it is as dramatic as day to night.

Society ...What Is It?

It makes me question society now, and we were just best friends, me and the interviewer and me and society. All I was doing was lending a hand to help a classmate; I guess he should not have been helped. That tells you to look at everything exactly the way it is, nothing else. It was his fault after all. It's just another example of how fast life just goes from day to night; all it took was a 10 minute meeting and a letter to my mother. They didn't even suspend me in person … They just sent a letter not even to the crib but to her directly. I didn't even know how that was possible. The worst part about all this was the person whom the bag belonged to was still in school-----IN HIS OWN DORM!

I capitalized the word *dorm* because he was as happy as he could be, and I think that he was able to finesse this situation because of that dorm at the end of the day. A dorm would have resolved all this. Not even resolve—they would have had no reason to suspect that bag of being mine if it were not in my dorm. I am writing this out, and it might do something for me one day, but this is really the only good way of getting my words out---that and therapy, which I will be attending tomorrow morning. My life will be back up soon... just under construction.

I'm just gonna basically hit a reset button and go back to therapy, work, and most of all, try to make this as if nothing happened and go back to school. If I were in a beautiful world, I would just go back to Curry in a dorm starting a brand-new Kijuan. Not even Curry if it were magnificent; I would be in a little apartment attending UMass Boston, which I should have started out doing. This is all just from me following signs. Maybe I needed to learn this and it could not be learned anywhere else. I hope this whole experience was just a lesson in God's plan because I went into this as blind as you could be … I didn't see this coming at all. I thought I was taking a slap on the wrist at most.

One thing I promise to do is right. As simple as that, I do the right thing. It is not like I am a bad person doing bad things all the time, but sometimes I just feel brave and want to do a little experiment. I am just getting extremely tired; I never had the energy to do this. I do not know where it came from. I believe it was from me being surrounded by so much energy at that school. I like to match the energy given. I feel it is how you go to college because believe me, there is a way. If I couldn't find the energy to be there, I wasn't, because I feel you can't.

For starters, I will be cutting this little Afro off my fade---Possibly grow it back, but hopefully not. This signifies a fresh start, a new start. It means a lot to me simply due to that. I will also be trying a different look, just adding to my attire. Instead of no headwear, I'll add a hat. It's a small change, but I feel it makes a big difference. That or waves because I need my head on spin sometime soon.

I believe a dorm would have avoided all these problems and be a way for me to grind out college in all aspects. I feel I was doing well and on my way up in school as a commuter. No one said anything to me, and I was getting all the help I needed, soon more. But once again, I am trying to take this whole situation as a lesson, but my mom just has the urge to make it difficult for me to come up the way I think was planned for me to come up. But I am going to let her rock. I don't have many obstacles, so let's see if I will get around this one. I think I will; I hope I do.

My mother even had the nerve to tell me I need to be in a home or rehab … Am I tripping, or would a dorm not solve all that as well? 'Cause I mean, I just need space. This is exactly why I stay in my room all the time. It is simply a place to think---either in quiet, watching television, or even listening to music. She said she chose the wrong words, but I'm gonna be in a dorm the same amount of time I would be away. Right? Or am I bugging? And that's all besides the fact that rehab is a place for people who abuse drugs, do absolutely nothing, or have a physical or even mental problem. I know I have my bumps and bruises, but nothing that serious. I do not believe so anyway. People tend to rock with me though, like the lawyer I went to see today for the previous accident I will get into later. He, of all people, gave my mom a compliment about me. That was not just any lawyer; you can walk in his office and tell he was no joke, and his office was in the city. I'm probably overthinking it, but it meant a lot to me.

I use the analogy "day to night" because I feel that life truly makes that dramatic difference, and I try to make my nights in life as fast as possible, and night tends to go quickly when you are sleeping. That means try to make life go by like a dream; it is harder than it seems though. For me, it's not just one big daze; it just involves a periodic high. Unfortunately, my nights in life are filled with nightmares. I cannot wait until I begin to be in the midst of a beautiful dream. In my daytime in life, figuratively, I love life, we are best friends, and I feel untouchable. I believe that was a problem for me when I was still at Curry because of what happened. I thought I could not be touched; I was chillin', stress-free, just getting work done, and smoking my weed.

Matter of fact, weed helped me drastically in college. When I had weed and energy, I was so focused. The professor had all my attention, possibly more. I think professors thought I was weird because I just stared at them and said absolutely nothing, might catch an answer every once in a while. Now saying that, I am medically certified, but I am not about to take a whole-ass thirty grams with me. Keep in mind that I am a commuter, so I'll be back home. Everyone knows I smoke the weed I purchase. I do not sell unless it happens to fall in my hands. Nothing crazy either, like a dim or dub at most, and THAT WAS NOT EVEN ON CAMPUS! I keep my bundle of weed at home where I feel it is safe. Cars get broken into or stolen. Houses do not get stolen unless it is the government or it's a mobile home. A house can be broken into, but that is the last safe place I can keep it, thinking I would not get into any sort of trouble. My weed didn't, but I did.

Okay, let me get into why I am medically certified. I was in a traumatic car accident. Well, traumatic for me. The driver broke his foot, maybe a couple scratches. It was traumatic for me because I ended up in a coma for a couple months. Now in that coma, my doctor said I passed a few times, and I was considered lucky to be alive. It was also traumatic for me because I came out of that situation

with a TBI (traumatic brain injury), which led to a few problems--
One being my eyes. They have a slight miscorrelation; it is called
adult strabismus, which will heal following surgery. Anyway, I am
medically certified because it seems to improve my focus and keep
me from thinking about what I have been through; in other words,
it helps with anxiety and depression. I mean, if you were to see me
a year or two after that accident, you would not believe that accident
happened if you did not see any permanent scars.

Visions

Another thing I did not talk about was what I saw during that two
month coma. Let me tell you, you could not maintain your perception
of what life was before something as dramatic as that happened. It
changed my view on everything. I have asked multiple people whom
I know would give valid answers to multiple questions just to see the
way they perceived life. I feel my perception is completely different,
and I'm hoping some of it is wrong because if I'm right, I am on
extremely thin ice. Just so it is clear, I stumbled, I took that in stride.
I did not fall and refused to fall. God got me; he is not about to allow
some nonsense like that to happen ---especially with the family,
friends, classmates, and community I have behind me. It is just up to
me to keep my head straight.

Looking back on my life, personally, I think it is hilarious. Things really started popping off when I was like eight. I still remember thinking I was a dare-devil and tryna hop a three-foot cliff on my bike doing my BMX thing. My face was destroyed. I had a permanent scar on my lip during my childhood and broke my shoulder, which coincidentally dislocated a few years later along with my ankle in a football injury. It just broke in a few places along with my shoulder. I have a big list of lessons learned, and I feel I might have had to learn some twice. It's fine though. I know them now, and I'm definitely not forgetting and trying my hardest not to repeat it. People are just looking at a prosperous Kijuan--- ON THE COME UP!

Some other lessons came from friends and family and did not require me getting hurt fortunately ---just through observation, seeing the way other people handled things and me thinking about what I would do if I were in that situation. Being in Quincy during my childhood and early adolescence was a key factor due to me spending a lot of time with a lot of interesting people consistently. I also spent elementary school in Georgia, so it made me, I guess you can say, diverse. I can conduct myself properly in various settings --- Just another reason why I believe God has a plan for me. When I go to other towns, I don't see kids doing the things I did as much as I should.

I feel those lessons were important because they will give me an idea or teach me how to handle similar situations in the future. One of a few lessons I have been taught now is that everyone you come in contact with cannot be your friend; it does not matter what setting you are in or what they do for you. They can change in the blink of an eye. This is something I feel everyone should experience in various ways because it also taught me to not get too comfortable and stay on my toes. I thought school was a place I could relax and not have to deal with real-world problems, but college gave me a relatively large real-world problem, still no match to some hospital visits though. See what I mean? Look what I'm going through and it is still no match to some of the other things I MADE it through. I capitalize *MADE* because of the situation where making it through was highly unlikely.

Another thing is people can't just let me rock. Like I think they see me being as happy as I can be, trying my best to mind my business, and people just find a way to ruin it. The last two major incidents were caused by two teenage white males. That's a problem because me and white people tend to get along. Half of my friends are white. I mean, I grew up in Quincy. Look at my high school lacrosse picture and you'll see exactly what I mean when I say that. Being black and playing lacrosse in Quincy should say everything itself, if you know anything about Quincy, Massachusetts or lacrosse in 2016. I don't want anything coming between the fact that I am chilling around the average white people, so I look at it as a small hurdle— some harder than others, but I get over them. It shouldn't even be about race; it just had to be like this, I guess.

I really do not know how I get over a good amount of these, but I am so thankful I do. I really believe that is due to me being meant for something, and I am determined to reach that meaning and do something incredible when I reach it. I hope these aspirations really mean something and they get done. They look like they will sometimes, and sometimes they don't. I feel a little glow inside whenever things look like they are going up, but when something dramatic happens, my aspirations crumble. I just have to build them up again, and it might just be different. Like I've gone from psychologist to sports psychologist to dispensary owner to author/ filmmaker. I'm definitely doing at least two of those things; it would be marvelous if all five happened and I was the sports psychologist who owns a dispensary and wrote a book that was also a movie. Life would be great. That's what I'm aiming for, so anything near it should not be a let down. Life thinks it is funny; hopefully the jokes end soon.

CHAPTER 2

Pain and Relief

If you know me, you might not. You would know I am a nice person as in I won't hesitate to help unless it is called for me to do so. You might see me slip every once in a blue moon, but I just gotta keep in mind that this is life. It does whatever it feels like doing or maybe whatever you provoke it to do. I don't think I have done anything to end up in a hospital or even be suspended from college. But guess what? When God pays me, it will be something nice. Because I'm not doing what most people would do—that is, just give up or just become a mean, stubborn person. God knows if I am in a position to give, I give with no problem. The only reason I do that is because I know those blessings will come back, possibly wealthier. I don't just do things to receive. I might just care about you or not want you in that situation. Like when I went to California, I was walking into CVS and saw a lady with two children outside with nowhere to go, and it was blazing hot. I didn't give them money because I didn't know their story in detail, but I just went and got them some water because that was what they asked for. I was with my uncle, and I could tell he was proud of that, and that made me feel so much lighter. It just gave me a feeling I cannot describe ---Especially after he said it.

Something I have also realized through the aftermath of all this is that my mother truly just wants the best for me. She just has a bad way of showing it. She doesn't want to let go, but I have to get things done as soon as possible, and a dorm will allow me to attend social events and feel more social in school, and that is one thing that leads to my completion ---Just because I can do things at the campus after dark and make friends while I'm getting my education, which is honestly how I think I got through high school. I had to make it fun for the eight hours a day and five days a week I was there. I think I was just trying so hard to make friends because I really didn't feel like I bonded with anyone there. I felt weird. It gets me mad that she really is trying to refuse me leaving, but I have to respect it. You have to see one of my many dilemmas.

Let me tell you, writing this out has helped me a lot just going throughout the day. I feel a more stable-minded Kijuan who has more knowledge behind his words, at times. I love it. I should be back in school by the time this gets published, if it does. But even when I'm there that just means more stories to add to my story. This book should honestly just reassure young people that adolescents everywhere are going through the same thing in multiple aspects. Just take your struggles and try to deal with them as smoothly as possible.

Now this is where the relationship part comes in... Listen, when I got out of the hospital, I was curious ---let me start by saying that. When I woke up from my coma, three days later, I was in a relationship. I was pretty stable until I got back to Quincy. Girls started hitting me left and right, so as the gentleman I am, I would just let them have it. I also tried to cut small talk short ---only to find out I have to just find that one girl who just feels amazing ANDwhom I have that sentimental/romantic connection with.

My problem with my last relationship was the fact that as I usually do, I wanted life to look as normal as possible coming from big incidents. On top of that, I gave people something else to talk about when my name came up. I don't know if that was smart or a stupid mistake, but I should make this a smart decision, as I told my friend, "Sex will carry more meaning, and I'll know what to do with it." I would definitely feel better; I feel like life will just all fall together once again, and I'll just try my best to mind my own business and focus on my work and, of course, handle the responsibility I have as a man. I feel I am going through this because of my eyes. I don't think I am an ugly dude. Keep it a bean. Am I?

Well, anyway, I hope to find a girl who can somehow look past this eye thing. I hope it goes away. I don't really see how that's possible, but I just gotta wait it out and keep my hopes up and have hope it gets better. That is another thing I am putting on my wish list for God. I will be there; that will be my baby. We are going on this mission together. "Teamwork makes the dream work." I feel like that could really be my only request ---well, that and the dorm. But that is the one thing I'm scared of; I get a girlfriend and my life falls apart. But it shouldn't because it didn't last time; I just gotta stay on track. It really shouldn't be hard. I think all the stupidity is out the window.

Since It's Thanksgiving

Since it is Thanksgiving, I will tell you what I am thankful for and how thankful I am for it. I am thankful for six things as of now: family, friends, life, money, and the people plus the things I have access to. Family because without them, I don't think I would have made it out of that hospital without their support and attention. My mom was there almost every day, and so was the rest of my family. Friends because they were there just as much as my family, and the doctors often said I was a well-cared-for kid. And once again, I believe that is because I am a nice person; no one expected it. Life because I mean … I'm breathing, I couldn't be happier because of that; I just want to breathe as comfortably as I can make it while I am doing it. I don't want this ending anytime soon. Money because I just have to place my attention somewhere, love or money. And things I have access to because I feel there are fellow kids and young adults who do not have these things. So I'm taking all the use I can of everything I can.

I want people to know about my life just so people won't feel that they are the only one going through it. It is all up to you whether it gets better or worse. I still believe the hand I was dealt was decent, even with all the things that happened or was going on. You just have to find something that you really want or need. Don't take your eyes off it, work for it, and you will receive it —possibly based on how hard you worked for it. If you were to grind for it, it may be beautiful. If you got it with a snap of the fingers, it may not be as beautiful.

Like if you were to work or somehow get your own money to buy your car, the car would mean more to you and you will feel more dependent on yourself.

I find it amazing how I could go through all this and still carry a smile on my face. I feel that is because of the way I was raised. Things get down, of course, but don't let them keep you down. I say that because I know people and stories where they would just dwell over that problem after they tried to fix it and fail. Keep trying; one time out of all the times you'd try will have to work. You just have to try, but try in various ways—keep that in mind. I'm not saying that all of it is done; I have things I am still dealing with. I'm gonna be dealing with it until it is resolved; I'll find a way.

And you know what? This is all my fault at the end of the day. I should never have got into that car with him or be negligent enough to understand what I was heading into when I was called for the meeting. I can't do anything about it now; I just can't look back. It happened; I learned from it. Stunts I'd pull—I felt them. Or trying any of the social tricks I attempted. I'll just be straightforward. By social tricks, I mean telling certain people certain things for a certain outcome, not the true outcome. I thought I was straightforward and honest in most aspects, so I mean, I thought I could afford to do those things. "What could happen to you Kijuan?"

I'm doing fine for the time being; January comes and it's back to work hopefully. As of now, I'm gonna do something in December with some friends who have been there for me and have not switched. I'm doing this because they have been working with me, helping me, and giving me motivation to go up. I don't think I would be doing some of the things I am doing without them. I just had to find a way to appreciate them. Hopefully they know I love them. This is also a way for me to celebrate being here ---just happy, something to celebrate.

A kid from Quincy just died around the same time and I almost died at the same age. These roads are dangerous right around now. It's been 2 years since the party, but let me chill out. I will have one, but it will have to wait. For now, let's see if I can do this. Because one person has already canceled on me.

The person from Quincy, just like me, recently passed in New Hampshire on I-93, and it reassured me a lot. One thing, most importantly, is that I am very blessed and fortunate to have survived something as traumatic as what I went through. This really tells me that I am meant for something —something above average. It just gives me the ambition I need to get it done; I need every bit of that as I can in order to do what I want.

Now that I think about it, the fact that people never bothered me or said anything to me does not mean I'm doing what I am supposed to do, when I'm supposed to do it, and how I'm supposed to do it. It is just the fact that people really just will not tell you about the things you do wrong. It's all up to you to do it and learn from it. I failed to realize that and just realized that yesterday when my manager asked me to do something. I did it and was continuing to do it, but one of the covers fell off the spatula. And I had placed it on top of the shelf in order to continue it later, but I saw in her face after she saw it that she was annoyed, and she just told me to stop. That could be because she had been there all day and was tired, but it just kept a flame under me.

Lessons

Something I learned tonight was something I knew for a while. No one told me, or I just don't remember; it was just not to let people think you have things or can do things. Just because they may take advantage of that ---well, not anyone and everyone. I did not really know that. I thought people just looked at me as someone they could become friends with. I am a friendly person. That is something that I think was a factor in my Curry situation. The friend I thought I could make looked at me as a free get-away card because of MY medical card, and it turned out some kid robbed him a few weeks later---not at gunpoint, but he took his weed, locked the doors, and drove off. Maybe that was the equivalent for that suspension from Curry. That kid robbing him means exactly what I believe; everything comes back one way or the other, good or bad.

Did you know there was a black young man shot in the mall with a gun who was trying to stop a guy shooting up the mall? He was even in the military, and a security guard shot in the back of a bar, and he was just trying to stop a fight. It is not like it is all happening now; it has been happening, but no one truly knows how to fix that factor. I just find it unbelievable that it is getting that common to shoot a black person. On the brighter side, I applied to UMass Boston; my application is just pending now. People have begun to bring back-up plans, and I really hope I don't need one. My first plan is first for a reason, and I never had a third school in mind ---maybe Eastern Nazarene just to avoid the fear I have of driving on highways, which has got better though. I coincidentally got on the highway and really did not mind; it was smooth. But hopefully UMass Boston goes as planned and I can complete my next moves. It feels like they will as of now, but just like before, that could change in a second. I'll add Eastern Nazarene and give it a shot.

Something else I learned while I had my time with someone who means the most to me is to take notice of the fact that I am actually doing this with different father figures. I say that because I am pretty sure it is particularly popular to know your father growing up in America, in this part of the country anyway. Well, at least I think so with all the dads I see around. I used to just think about having MY dad when I see a dad. In other words, I do not know my biological father. and I believe I am doing exceptionally well with that factor in my life. I think I am done with all that now, and that is relieving, but I really could not let that break me if something happened. That is because I care about my future a lot, and I am aiming for my life to be as close as I picture it, if not closer. I believe it is all about determination. I do not know where it came from, but I just want nice things so badly, possibly replace the fact that I do not know my dad. My mom is going to try to make it a big deal when she reads this and just say something to make me feel bad for it, but it is whatever to be honest. It is not like I do not have a father figure at the moment; I do. It is just the fact that I really have no clue who my father is. And I'm here once again with a smile on my face.

If someone is three. Do they know what they are asking for? I believe so, because I don't believe I was asking for things I didn't want when I was three. I say that because when one of my sisters was three, she didn't ask for anything she didn't want. I believe I had just as much common sense as her ---maybe even more. Now is it your fault when you comply with a three-year-old's wishes? Even if you just took it as a joke and did it without thinking of it again. As I suggested before, the dorm is a beautiful idea. Apparently, that has been the plan now, but did I say anything about a dorm being planned to have at UMassBoston? I don't think so. It's coming to the point where I need to leave. No one is even trying to view my perspective.

In Action

I talk about these things as they happen so it provides facts, not things I think I remember or fogged memories; it also helps me deal with whatever I'm going through at the moment. This is basically me just typing angrily because of something someone is doing. It's ridiculous that I have to do this, but it is relieving. My mom sent me to my grandmother's house, so I just had to let that rock because she took my keys and lied to me, saying she didn't have them and telling me my grandmother had them. Turned out she didn't, and watch this … My mom said my grandma had a copy. When I asked, she simply said, "What are you talking about?" Another lie. She lied three times in one night, and she hadn't lied to me in twenty years. Why is everyone doing me as dirty as they want? Did I do something wrong? If so, let me know.

Another thing I don't understand is how you send someone away when he really doesn't do anything else but work, go to school, or smoke? I could understand if I was belligerent or an all-around bad kid, but really, is anyone complaining about what I do in the household? Because I really haven't heard a thing. "Get your inspection sticker renewed"---that's all I have heard, and I just started hearing it three days ago. And it's not like I have been doing nothing for the past three days. I went to work and went to the gym ---mind you, that is just three days. Let alone me trying to get back into school and just figuring all that out last night. I go on Wednesday to get my common app submitted. People acting like this stuff is light at this age with what I'm coming from really does grind my gears, but I learned not too long ago to just let them rock. I really can't do anything else to my own mother.

And soon as I'm getting somewhere in my relationship aspect of life, this happens. I guess it's right when people say, "You can't have it all." But I want it all, and I don't think I'll ever stop trying to get it all. I'll just be the happiest Kijuan I've seen in a good little minute. Like before this girl even had the opportunity to come in the picture,

I wasn't saying anything to my mom and my mom wasn't saying anything to me. I didn't ask because I really didn't have the time and energy to deal with that. I carry just enough energy to get what I need to be done and mind my business. I've learned distributing unnecessary energy only ends with unwanted trouble. I don't want to deal with this. But guess what? I am.

After a good amount of time thinking about it. I thought it may be good that this is happening; maybe school is about to hop back on track. Relationships with girls may come back into play. I just have to play my cards right. If everything goes the way I have planned, over the next year, I'll be so grateful. Because I'm already thankful. This is how I see myself in a year; in Boston with a roommate and attending UMass Boston with my girl who is most likely attending UMass Boston, just living as happy as I can be getting everything done. I won't ruin it this time. This just basically means that if I don't know you or have connections with you or to you, do not be a bother. I might meet some people, but we will most definitely have things in common to ensure our friendship.

Another thing I want to talk about while I'm thinking about it is my stress level. People really don't seem to understand that I have lost my life due to a car. I have to drive a car everywhere I need to be. That is a responsibility I have as a young adult. That stress builds up after the days are over. And on the days I have to drive a lot, the stress is pretty high. I just make the most of it ---make it into positive energy. Something I need may keep the headaches away, which I feel coming as I type this. I don't get headaches, so this might be from lack of sleep —which I doubt because it is only 12:30 a.m. and I stay up far later than this ---or stress from the little attitude my mom is trying to catch with me. I think it is from that, but hopefully it is gone tomorrow. That's crazy. I went to the gym today, I should feel great. Instead I feel like this.

A little deeper into this thought process, my mom never once mentioned a dorm at UMass Boston. I went to Curry because I do not know any commuters attending that school. I know at least a few commuters attending UMass Boston. That is one reason I attended Curry. I thought my chances of dorming were higher. Moral of the story is, I am just trying to get away. It really should not be that much to ask for. I mean, kids from the wealthiest families go to dorms in college, and they are the kids who truly have everything. You know why? That is simply just to get away---nothing more, nothing less.

This is really helping me because after being sent to my grandmother's house, I just accepted it, came here, and started typing. I got through a quick ten paragraphs with ease, and I do not believe they are just talking trash about my mother. All this commotion is simply due to complying to something a three-year-old suggested. She has common sense. She knows what she wants. If she didn't want me doing it, she wouldn't ask. It is not like anyone is forcing her to ask. When I received whippings for a proper term, I didn't ask. It just doesn't make sense. And to make it worse, I remember a five paragraph essay I would write as punishment in second grade. This is not punishment to me. This is relief. Now I don't know if this should go down in history as a diary or a book after this case, but it stores knowledge, so I believe it may be a book.

I recently saw something on Twitter saying, "What has 2018 taught you?" And it has taught me a few things I should take note of ---that is, not everyone can be your friend, three-year-olds are basically talking out of their ass at the end of the day, and keep your head on a swivel. Everyone can't be your friend because look at the very first group of friends I made in college. Look what they got me into. Three year-olds are talking out their assed because look at what my sister got me into, originally as a joke. And keep your head on a swivel because anything can come at you from any direction it feels fit. So I feel if you take anything from my story, it should be to keep your head on a swivel because that works in all aspects.

CHAPTER 3

Struggle of Adversity

My mom says I am disrespectful or I speak to her as if I am speaking to one of my friends. She is wrong there because I tend to use slang or a solid amount of foul language with them because I can express myself freely as I please. The only way I can see me being disrespectful is by being right. That is absurd because we will be talking and I can be proving points and she'll just stand there and shake her head wondering where she went wrong as if she could have possibly gone wrong. Keep in mind that I still do not know my biological father and it means nothing to me---well, at least I don't want to find out if it does. I lost interest.

My mom is back on her shit a whole-ass day later. I need someone to tell me. Am I actually doing too much? I think doing less is impossible because I only do what I have to do and nothing else. Now she wants to say, "Oh, it's time for a dorm," like yo... did I not just say that shit? It's all I have wanted to do, and it took this much for it to be done. I like for things to be smooth, and now she wants to be extra. It took a whole extra couple yards just for me to simply move in a dorm or apartment. She's gonna sit here and try the same shit she tried last night, send me to my grandmother's house. That really won't work anymore. I have smartened up after last time; I did a lot of thinking.

And no one is telling me that they work harder than me---- Not in a physical aspect because that may be true. But mentally, I am worn. The voice in my head telling me to give up is small, so I choose not to listen to it. Let's hope this voice does not get any louder due to how much the stuff I'm dealing with means to me. I need to do it; that's that. People just love to be in my ear. I would say 25/8, but sometimes I think people just say, "All right, he's going through it. Chill out on Kijuan." But no, not right now. Hopefully, and I say this all the time, this is the last one. Most likely because I am young and writing a book, but let's take it easy. It's not like I just said, "If I change in this aspect, maybe it will help others." Like no, this just started happening. I've been doing the same thing for the past few months, and now it's, "Go to Nana's house." Like aw man, I really hope I get the dopest gift after dealing with this. Every year, it's one thing, if not the other. Next year is me leaving the house once again---for good. I can see it now. Low-key I want it, but I don't know if I can handle it.

My mom makes me feel as if no other kid is like me, which is true, but the average twenty-year-old is in his or her dorm and living as happy as they can be and the parents at home are living as happy as they want to be. I really do not know what is so difficult. I ask questions that make everything makes sense, and she refuses to reply to them. Like she just refuses to look at another aspect, and as a parent, I think it is very important to look from both aspects and weigh out the good and bad on both sides ---not just attach yourself to something you know was gonna have to leave and wait until you get angry or fed up with something and want them gone. She was doing so well but could not change when I changed. I believe we can figure this out. We are just gonna have a lot of headaches going through this, and I don't get headaches.

This may be because I had a good childhood and hopefully will have many good years after this. I'm just in my grind period. I've done it before, so it can get done. You really can't have it all in a lot of aspects. I guess I can say I lived a good life and am living a good life—minus all the bumps and bruises. But like I said, I'm here, and I can't be prouder. I just don't believe you can literally live a completely perfect life. You have to struggle at some point in some way for something. It sucks, but just make them as bearable as you can. I really cannot wait until I can just relax, chill out, just be free, and do what I want or need when I want.

My Thoughts

I can only stand to think of how my life would have been if I did not get into that accident. I do not know where I would have gone, but lacrosse most likely would still have been a factor in the school I was going to, and that would have forced me to dorm, considering that I really do not believe I would have been smoking as much as I do --- due to the fact that I would not have my medical card and I don't think I really wanted to in the first place. I just realized it helped more than it hurt me, but I played sports. That is something I learned while I was up there. It is not for anything bad; it is grown for a reason. Especially if you are not doing anything athletic; I mean, I have started working out, but I don't run that much, just weight lifting. I need to. I just need to sweat, so I wear a sweat suit in order to sweat when I go to the gym more than when I wear shorts or something. But anyway, I don't know what route I was really taking. I just know college was a factor. I was not doing terribly in school, average; math was hard, so it brought it down. But I did well in history and, ironically, English, Science got a little shine. I do remember that I was highly interested in psychology, so it would have been in that field—but not sports psychology specifically. Knowing me, I would have found a way to get money coming in because that means something to me now; it gives things purpose. I wish I could watch what my life would have been like. It would be amazing.

After writing that, I spent a lot of time thinking about what I would have been aiming for in the psychology field if none of this did happen. I think I would have been more interested in children and adolescents in psych because I deal with that enough in life with my sisters, and that is probably a small battle to some other teens who have way bigger problems, like not having a place to call home or not even someone to call a mom or dad. That sounds tough, and it takes a certain mindset to get through something like that; you have to be very strong-minded to get through something like that. I would love to help children, teens, and anyone with a brain injury. If I can be everything I aspire to be, I'll be content with my life---even with all the injuries, just a part of childhood.

I do not know if this will be considered a book or a journal, but honestly, a journal is a book. I do not go by day, so I myself do not consider this a diary---more as a book of knowledge to humble whatever experience you are going through. Just keep in mind that the older you get, more people have more stories. And they may just be unbelievable, but they happened. Hopefully they themselves and you make it through whatever you are going through. Because believe me, it sucks. A lot of people take a loss and sit down, but not me. I may need a break, or I may not even need that. You just need to forget your faults at a fast pace. Something else I believe is true is that every visionary is ridiculed before they are properly acknowledged. That is why I am writing this book. People will say, "Oh, he's twenty This book shouldn't mean much," but this book should help you or humble you once you read it.

My uncle said one mistake cannot ruin your life, but my mistake got me kicked out of college and my other mistake got me ejected out of the passenger side door. The only way I plan to survive is to start out in college then work my way up. Let's hope this is very true because honestly, what else could I be? That makes good money anyway. Also somewhat broke down how he came up, almost went to jail, not too clear how but I heard it had something to do with some girl. Now he's working to make $20,000 a month. I'm tryna have that and more if I can help it. I still believe it will happen; I have my hope and determination. He smokes weed too, not as much as me but he also does not have his medical card. People really need to stop deterring weed because he smokes weed and he's going up, I smoke weed and I'm writing a book … like really, weed does not slow you down until you do it too much and you are in a particular sport or doing anything that requires persistence. It is on its way to recreational use, but if it has had these effects for years, it should have been sooner.

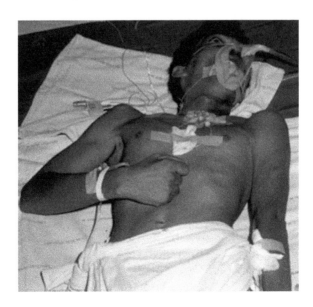

Anything can portray your future. That's the funny thing about life, even music. I listen to a lot of positive music, and I hope it is telling me something about my future. I also listen to some trap music, but I mean, music is also music. That means there are multiple types of music to choose from and you can choose any type you like. I happen to like trap, some trap music. That does not take away from the fact that I do listen to a lot of positive music by positive artists. Listening to music and speaking to my uncle, I realized one thing: Life has seasons just like the weather. You have good sunny days, and you have those bad rainy days or however you look at it.

I don't believe you understand what I'm about to do when and if I get into UMass Boston. I'm definitely taking creative writing now because I feel it will be extremely interesting to me now due to me writing this book. It will give me ideas, and I will have the proper people around me to get this book somewhere. I may try the double major just because I'm looking at all the money I'll make out of both of those aspects with them combined. It's a long shot, but this one is a special shot. I just have a few questions because if I double-major, it will be business and psychology; I'll figure it out. I'll take up business just because I would like an idea of what to do in the business world.

Trying to Go Positive

If you take away all the negatives in my life that I wrote about in this book, there would still be small problems that are just going to float, like people lying to me. My friends used to lie to me, but they were just people I socialized with because I was in school. Some do more than others, but family members just say small lies. I guess because they don't mean much. They could be mistakes, but it has been happening a lot, and that's worrisome. But I really do not have time to deal with it, so I can deal with it.

I learned that when you are going to dorm, you don't need a long story to explain why you want to dorm if you do. Just four simple words in my case: "I just need space." It sounds like a lie if anyone who just met me were to hear my story because honestly, who is going to believe it? Even though every part of my story is 100 percent true, these words are something anyone and everyone should understand.

When I say, "Take that L in stride," I mean you should not let that failure in your life stop you. Find the next best way around it. I'm sure there is one, but there may not be. I also say that because I believe I can support it. Look at all the Ls I've taken; one of them almost caused me my life. It's okay. I tried not to let that slow me down; it paused my life at best. I really have so many to note, but I do not want to just write how many things I failed to do in life because I didn't fail; I learned and conquered. I believe that is fair to say.

After talking about all the things I did wrong, let's talk about some of the better things that make me who I am today. I played football and lacrosse. I played football through all of my childhood and some of my teenage years. I believe it gave me a work ethic and aspirations; it also helped a lot in my accident because my brain adjusted to trauma well. Then I played lacrosse the first three years of high school, where I was the first black lacrosse player to score in that sport at Quincy High School. It sort of gave me a shape as well. It would have been four years if it were not for that accident, but let us not start that again. Lacrosse honestly opened my mind; it made me want to try some things and step out of my comfort zone. My mom pitched the idea. I got the Principal's Award after graduating the same year that took place. That meant a lot to me because that was hard and well deserved, and it showed me that people saw that, and they had me with the Best Smile senior year. I believe that was also because of the accident and because I smiled a lot. I like to be happy, so I will just let that rock. I had a few more things, but I will not let this begin to be about all my accomplishments either. I believe those accomplishments are the reason why I expect myself to do so well in life. I mean, bad start, but I am almost there.

Once again listening to music, I thought about something else I had to do that was ridiculous during my stay at Curry. I had to sleep on the floor of someone else's dorm, another factor in my suspension. Like I said before, if I had my own dorm, they would have had no reason to suspect that bag of being mine. It still does not take away from the fact that the bag actually was not mine and I was two hours away doing something for Netflix during this discovery; they might have just been hating, which is odd.

I went to UMass Boston today to start my process of transferring there. I liked the facility and the people in the facility, but I liked Curry's facility at first sight too, so I just have to stay on my toes with that, which means I just have to be cautious. My mom told me not to go in because they wouldn't help me, but guess what? They even gave me the waiver to avoid having to pay for my application. I knew I wanted to go for a reason, and that was one in particular of a few that made me really appreciate what I was doing because it gave my mom a little sense of humanity, if she realized or not.

After writing this, I asked my mom if she realized they actually were helpful, and she said, "Yes, but every school does not do that." That may be true because Curry was not helpful whatsoever. I tried to make them helpful, and they were on the road to becoming helpful, and that happened. Every other school may not be as helpful, but I am not concerned about them. I am just focused on UMass Boston in particular.

I think it is amazing how I still have faith in humanity. That may be because they got me through something as traumatic as what I was going through and a few other minor things. I feel you need it and you get it by making things possible for other people. It just makes it more of a possibility. I'm not saying that they made me come out of that because I made them able too, but I trusted them. and so did my family. Any doubt would have made it much harder for them to do what they did for me.

My therapist made me realize today that there are two ways you could take the weed route: you can either make millions out of it or you can end up in jail or end up suspended from college like me (and it wasn't even my weed). I mean, that is a big difference honestly. You could have nothing or have everything at the end of the day if the only thing you are interested in is weed. I think it is hilarious that the same thing people are making legal money out of, people are going to jail for and lead to me getting suspended from college.

In order to do these things without being affected by them is simply not to think about them; get them done as soon as possible. That way it won't weigh too much in your head. "The longer you wait, the more it weighs." That is so true because I've put things off, so I'm not gonna act like I do not do it. I'll just try my best not to do it as frequently as I did. My life has gone a tad bit smoother; there were a few boulders, few pebbles, but I think I'm done with those. UMass Boston seemed welcoming, but I have learned not to judge too quickly. It was love at first sight with Curry; I thought it was meant for me. Things were going so well, but anyway, just try to be quick to forget or use it as fuel to get over it, one or the other.

CHAPTER 4

Be Quick to Forget

I know that "Be quick to forget" sounds impossible if something as traumatic as what happened to me or this college situation happened to anyone, but once you are over it, don't look back. I don't talk to anyone about that accident or the fact that I am suspended from college simply due to that. I got through that accident thankfully, and I'm getting over this college mishap just as smooth as I got into it. Now I got that done through determination, keeping God with me, and ambition. As long as those are straight, you are straight.

Almost

Now that weed is legalized, I feel free to promote weed if you have a medical card or are over twenty-one. Weed has been so great to me and what I have had to go through. I can just accept it and work to make others accept it. I feel if I didn't smoke, I would be incredibly mad at my life. I'd probably want to kill myself. I am just thankful I do not have those feelings right now, and I hope I do not ever get the feeling that it would have been best if I died. I tried to say it, but I couldn't bring myself to actually believe it.

One song I want to sing proudly and believe is "Never Lose" by Meek Mill. I bring this up because I feel like I will get to a point where I just come out on top of everything and lose it all. I do not do anything to anyone to have this stuff happening to me, but I just lose. I am determined to get to a point in my life where I can sing that song and mean it permanently. I will know because I will just get that feeling I get whenever something meaningful happens.

I believe small things that happen to me in life and take much more pride, which pushes me to go higher. It has not hurt me, and I hope it doesn't hurt me. One thing that has hurt me is my sympathetic side, which I will not leave; there is a mistake in everything and everyone. Just because I had sympathy for a fellow weed smoker doing what he had to do in school, when I say that I'm saying, I'm a helpful person and a helpful spirit was behind me. I feel like I'm coming back just as smooth, but we will see what they say tomorrow.

That accident really boosted my ambition so much; it is honestly crazy. A few months after getting out of the hospital, graduating, and getting college set, I had three jobs. My mom doesn't like to call it three because one was in a gym and another was a campsite but were both under the YMCA so two jobs---take or leave three. The other job was Champs, and then that turned into Lids Locker Room fairly quickly. I like the Lids Locker Room, the store and the people I work with. I just hope they like me. I was doing all that because I had to place my time somewhere and I had to make money to afford weed. So I spent my time making money. I just got my hip to society slowly but surely. I got to talk to people, see different people, and see a lot of different things, believe it or not.

After that period of me just working, I took a break after, I would say, a year---close to a year---but then again, you can say I was forced to. I quit my campsite job but coincidentally got fired like a week later from the gym. I got my money out of them, and I recently started going to the gym again. I still work at Lids, and hopefully that won't be changing anytime soon. My manager is cool, and she works with me, meets me halfway. I have to respect it.

After thinking about it, I believe UMass Boston has been a set school for a good amount of time before this setback happened, and I received a TBI now after, and I had my mind set on Curry. That is why I believe all this is a plan, and it gets me so hyped. Let's just hope I am not pumping myself up and something actually happens. It's three in the morning, and I am lying here typing this. I believe that is all I need to say. Off a simple thought too.

A lot of things come back to that accident. That's the only reason I bring it up as much as I do. It messed up my brain dramatically, and you have to understand how hard I had to work to get past that. I believe I made that go a tad bit smoother, so I made it look easy. But trust me, if people had to go through that, people would already understand, so I wouldn't have to elaborate as much as I did or will.

Mindsets

You can have a goal or a mind-set to get that goal. Success is one way to come out of achieving that goal. You can also be depressed hoping that achievement would be special or more special than you thought. The success of that goal shows that you are dedicated, smart, and loyal to that goal. People have failed to achieve their goal due to them letting minor setbacks contradict their future or take control of their actions. The worst thing to do is give up or "take a break." I quoted "take a break" because some people will say that and fail to continue their process.

When you are young, you don't have a fear of what you are going to learn; you don't have time to sit and think about it. As you get older, you will lose the interest to learn, so I suggest you do as much as you can while you still want to. Pretty soon it will be "Been there, done that," but if you carefully learn anything that falls into your hands as a child, you will find that you will be a tad wiser in that particular subject.

I find psychology interesting because I want to know how people think and why people think the way they think. I recently picked up an interest in business because I plan to open a business and want to know how things will work when I get there. I wish I gathered these interests earlier, but I was just looking more toward sports. I had a regular child's dream of playing football or lacrosse somewhere for someone. I knew I wasn't gonna do anything big, but I could have played in college. I had been playing sports for far too long not to.

I will try and double-major now because my love for psychology has not left and I need to know the aspect of business because everything revolves around it. That is also a step in having everything I want come true. I am not trying to be the smartest or to know it all; I just need to know enough. I've seen people who know everything, and I have seen people who know enough, and I know the difference. Well, I think I do. I believe people who just know enough or a bit more are far happier, but I may see some different people at UMass, most likely. I probably will minor in business, so we'll just have to see.

After putting my thoughts or problems down in writing, I just feel lighter or weigh less until the situation is handled, another example of how things weigh more the longer they sit on your head. I feel good; I feel more confident. I just feel more at ease with things like my friends coming over and one of them deciding to sit in my spot- -- eventually lying in my bed with his shoes off because he was not about to lie in my bed with shoes on. I was completely content with that, and that made me feel like I was getting somewhere. That usually would have been a big deal, but not recently.

I try to be as politically correct as possible, so to be politically correct, I am trying to choose a college route and set my life exactly the way I want it to be or make the best of a political standard. I feel like I am preparing for takeoff right now, because we are going up. Hopefully I set everything up perfectly and this is a smooth hurdle. I've been cruising, but I can lose control at any moment. I promise if I get where I need to be, I will not disappoint.

"You either become where you are from or make something out of it." That says a lot about kids everywhere because they can become a negative statistic, not even be considered for a statistic, or make it out and do something positive. I came up well; I'm not saying I came from the trenches, but I want more than what I have. That should say a lot, should show you how much this means to me. I could be content with this, and I am, but I want to say, "I did it better than some expected."

Sometimes you just have to go somewhere quiet and just relax and think. Plot your way through each problem you are dealing with carefully, implement those thoughts, and get back to me with how you feel after because I have felt great and it was indescribable. I think I tend to work for things for that feeling and the prize; it is a combo for me.

If you are a good person and you bring that up repetitively, are you considered a good person? I think if you do things out of kindness and rarely bring it up, that is fine. If you constantly bring up the fact that you are a good person, it becomes annoying. I find it sort of offensive because I know you did it. Maybe after some time and you needed something. People try to take advantage of that, but you just have to learn the difference between friendly and too friendly. After learning that again, I do feel a lot better going through life; things have gone the way I needed to outside of the house.

As far as life goes inside of the house, all I can say is we are moving. We're still waiting on a go-ahead so we can move in, but we are in the prep stage. Let me tell you something else. The stage I am in right now may be the hardest. I do not remember moving, and maybe it is due to my doctors saying I would have low energy, but I think it is pointless. You don't know how much space you will need until you use it.

I believe it is a privilege to be alive. I say that because I cannot imagine a world without me; I don't mean that in a sarcastic way. I made the best of every situation I entered and was able to control. I believe it does not matter who you are; you just have to make the best of that person. It is a privilege to be alive because I mean … you are here, so make the most of it. Give your life meaning, big or small. I have ambitions to give my life a big meaning. I hope these ambitions turn to reality.

I do not believe my ambitions are too high. I just would like to live a comfortable life and try to get things sturdy enough to hold together. Once that happens, I still will not get off my feet because who knows what other issue can come next. Hopefully my God or life in general will give me a break. I am not asking for anything too big or extravagant but also nothing too small. I think I am asking for just enough; I feel as if I will live just as comfortably as I'm living now financially.

Simply focus itself should be the reason you prosper. It may take more but also may give you more reasons to want it. Focus is, I guess you can say, tunnel vision. Try your best not to let things get in the way of that vision, and I am a perfect example. Anything can happen. I have to respect it because I feel I'm being put through this because I am going somewhere, so I'm not complaining. Even if I don't do anything, I have faith in myself. I'll find a way to live comfortably, hopefully sooner than later. I think I'll have a smooth transition if UMass accepts me, anywhere else too. I'll most likely spend another semester at Quincy College, but hopefully not. I am trying to get a plan I have in mind into action; it will be beautiful.

How?

When or if you get there, just stay humble. Me getting up, loving life, and some nonsense coming into the picture like it was welcome has happened too many times. All I can do is think and laugh about what life has thrown at me; hopefully I can keep laughing after or there is an after. It is the worst thing; you spend the day after, if not days, thinking, *"Why?"*, *"What did I do?"* You just have to realize shortly after that you have to get back to where you were and act like nothing happened. It gives you a story as a person and gives you something to say you prospered out of.

I think there is one thing I never forgot with my mindset and stature. Don't get your hopes up too high; just aim for positivity. Saying that, I just never had dreams of becoming a professional football player or anything too out of reach for me as a person. You might have caught me saying something about lacrosse at the time, but nothing crazy. I believe if you create morally or physically possible ambitions, you are more likely to achieve your goal. I think I am meant for psychology because life has given me a story to tell and sport psychology because I've been playing sports throughout my childhood and teenage years and I'm curious of some people's mindset in that setting and interested in knowing what they deal with and how to deal with it. Business because I would like to endure the aspect and create a dispensary of medicinal and perhaps recreational marijuana, hopefully in Quincy Center. I feel it will make a lot of money there because I've heard people say, "Quincy is the next Boston."

I think I found an answer to the reason this suspension all started. I was not even trying to, but I believe it was just because I was thinking I was on a college campus no one had an issue with anyone, no one was doing anything bad, and everyone was focused on their work. Sad to say, that was awfully wrong. You can't think that---maybe if you have known them in high school, but other than that, nah. I was trying to make best friends in months---that is, by making stories to remember, and that would have been a great story to remember.

I decided this is an educational book. It teaches you how to think while handling your situation, not how to handle it particularly but a step in the right direction. I say this because I explain my situation enough to understand; there is room for elaboration, but that is on purpose. After explaining what I went through, I said what I did to put it behind me. You just have to find a way to solve it and put it into action. Do not quit; try all your options.

I was watching an interview with Charlamagne tha God on the topic of mental health, anxiety in business, and relationships. One thing stuck out to me in that interview, and it was the point that if you are living a comfortable life and everything runs smoothly, you won. I really believe that, and I don't know how much I can tell you, but I really want to win. This is one game I can't lose; I've had my fair share of losses. Toward the end of me, I just want to sit back and be as happy as I can be and as wise as I should be. I want to do what I love and have my friends and family with me, perhaps a wife, a dog, a house, and a car.

Be friendly with people, but not too friendly. Keep your distance. I bring this up because it is so important as you get older. Do not let people know everything, but do not say nothing; you still must be heard. My grandmother brought that up to me, so I sat and thought---not too long because I think I have found all the answers I will find and hopefully choose the right one. Just don't let people know the details of your life specifically. It causes confusion. It is not hard to know the difference, but I am a generally nice person---perhaps too nice at times, but I have to control it, and I believe I have learned. I have seen some benefits.

Now I can't sit here and say that I do not have a day where I'm down or not in the mood to do something. It happens to everyone. Sometimes I can smoke and it will pick me up, but sometimes you can't do that, so I just make an agreement and calm myself. I typically feel better, then my knees will just start hurting from standing at work so long, not my feet, my knees. I really do not know why because I exercise, so I should have healthy knees. That is beyond me. That would have me ready to leave, but it doesn't alter my attitude, so I can still conduct myself as an employee.

You have to have the mindset to want to get better. Do not think it will just fall together; implement the work toward that goal. Always try to be a better you. Saying that, do what you can do and then do more; push yourself. Keep your future in mind. Always think of ways to get ahead years from now. You never know when the opportunity may be attainable. Just take moments to sit and examine your failures to learn from them. Find ways to avoid failure. Find something you are passionate about, like how I chose psychology as my first passion, which became sports psychology then business. If I get a shot at any of those possibilities, I will give it my all every day.

"Rest in the end, not in the middle." That is one quote from Kobe Bryant's English teacher Mr. Fisk. It just means that you put your work in now and embrace all the benefits at the end. You will really be thankful you did that. You have to keep a picture in your mind of something to strive for. You will just find yourself wanting it more depending on what it means to you. For me it is to have a family and a well-paying job with a nice house and car. If you do the things I said, I feel you will achieve the desire of being great. You will just find yourself holding your head higher with more pride unintentionally.

You have to have a plan to get all those things done. You must know step-by-step what you are doing. Sometimes you may need to improvise. Find leverage; in other words, find a key to get what you want and to open whatever you want to get into. Be proud of yourself, be proud of what you do. Carry a smile on your face each and everywhere you go. You do that by living your dream. You can't be mad in a dream, maybe scared in a nightmare. As long as you seize legal positive opportunities that benefit you now or anywhere in the future, you should be content with what you do.

Evolving

Try your best to evolve at all times. You have to get bigger one way or the other. Why not both? If it's sports for you, get your weight up. If you like to work in an office, get your knowledge up. Don't give yourself a headache, and you will be amazed by some things you learn that you can do. As long as you are loyal to your hustle and grind, then your hustle and grind will be loyal to you. You have to show it attention. As long as you are showing your hustle attention and getting things done in a timely manner, your grind should reimburse you greatly.

CHAPTER 5

Show appreciation

Appreciate what you do have and make use of it. Like I do not have everything, but I make use of everything I do have to make it seem like I have everything. You have to focus on what you do have to get what you don't have. As long as you are able to improvise, you will be a great businessman---like I texted the former mayor of Quincy's wife in an attempt to start the publishing of this book. I met her through a summer camp, and somehow I know her son. If you believe in what you're doing, it makes it that much more likely for it to come true. In any path you choose to take in life, I think it is extremely important to stick to yourself and keep control of who you are no matter how far you make it.

If you have to, start small and work your way up. Form a store out of the items you sold out of your backpack or something like that. Plan your actions carefully before you put that action into motion. You can dig yourself into a deep hole or even get yourself out of a hole. Finding something and someone you love is a key to enjoying your life in every aspect. You can come home to who you love and leave who you love to go do what you love every day. Imagine how happy you will be.

I come from humble beginnings. I believe that is why I am so even-minded. I see both sides or both aspects to everything. That is due to me living in both walks of life, meaning I can conduct myself well in the best of the best or worst of the worst. And spending my childhood in Georgia has just taught me that people really live completely different lives in completely different settings and carry different mindsets. It is amazing to see the way the society you live in makes you conduct yourself. Like my brother from Georgia whom my mother signed up for is a teacher and someone I like to call my brother went to jail. They came from relatively similar settings. Even though we have gone different walks of life, at the end of the day, we call one another brothers.

Bringing up jail also helped me remember a conversation I had with my friend Chris. He just got out of jail, and it was so unexpected that he went to jail. I do not know the logistics of his reasons for jail time, but it shows how fast life can change on you. My homeboy was driving around in a Benz, and he just graduated. I didn't think anyone could touch him, but they tried to find some reason. He got out months later thankfully, but that was honestly crazy.

In order to set or make accompaniments, a good way to go about that is to set daily goals. You achieve more, but not simple goals; challenging yourself can only show yourself a better you. Challenge yourself to do things that you think you cannot do with good reasoning. Things as small as that could give you better self-esteem and make you more aware of yourself. That could lead to a better life. You will feel more confident when talking to a significant other or simply get what you want just by speaking up.

Time to Party

I got my Airbnb to show all my friends the respect they deserve for showing me how much they care and to celebrate the fact that I am still here. It really is a shame that I would have to celebrate something for that, but this is the best possible way to show my excitement. You may not understand where this is coming from if you have not come close to death, but it is an unexplainable feeling. You may not realize it, but you just feel different---stronger---or even just feel as if you have the ability to do almost anything.

We had the party, and it went fairly successful. The parents came up once, but we were done, so that went by smoothly. It is three fifty in the morning, and I still have yet to get something I have been craving. I'm going through the meanest drought of this decade, and it is heartbreaking. I've seen people having sex and heard people having sex. That is ridiculous. I really do not know what I'm doing wrong. I mean, I have opportunities, I'll be working toward them, then something or someone just comes along and snatches it from me. That is honestly so depressing. If I were getting girls left and right, I would be more of a lenient person---even if I found one girl. But I get this life for a reason; I'm going to keep telling myself that.

I can only bear to think what my pay will be like when the tables turn. I really hope it is great. I don't believe anyone else goes through this. It's impossible. I really do not understand how I do this one but I do it. I mean, it's really insane when I think about it. Hearts out to all the people in the exact same situation I'm in because it is truly the hardest thing you can do. It takes a lot of heart and resilience when you take into account that you just threw a party and didn't get anything but a good amount of your friends did, even had friends telling you they would try their best to get you some tolerable form of female. I swear I can remember not even having to throw parties and getting some.

I guess I'm too friendly too soon. Like I'm a pretty low-key person when I first meet you, but after a few conversations, I may just like talking to you. Now when I say that, I mean I'll just have a smile on my face and ask more questions just to get to know you. I bring this up because when my mom paid some people to move our stuff when we were at the original house, a conversation came up about smoking and it turned out we both liked to smoke. About forty-five minutes to an hour later, I went downstairs and put together a little blunt, and he happened to come down, and I met the person he came with and had a nice conversation about nothing serious either, just like where you work and stuff. Then we went to the new house. And I had just picked up a few grams, so we smoked, and I gave him my number. My uncle thought that was too soon considering his appearance. I thought that was a bad way to think, but it was making me think. I did not know whether to completely disregard him or give him a shot. His appearance was a little off because he had no license and had two kids at twenty-six. Two kids at twenty-six did not bother me, but it was the fact that he had no license and was working off Craigslist that did it. No one knew who he truly was.

After throwing that party, I just felt like it was over, and it made me realize a lot. That was because people who weren't even on the list came, but I couldn't care because I had to do that sometimes, so I had to respect it or I'd be a hypocrite. That is the wrong thing I need said about me as a man who sees both perspectives of a lot of things because it is easy to confuse them. People will call you a hypocrite for saying things but doing something a tad bit different, possibly for a different outcome. That is why I continue to ask the question why.

I think I figured it out; it is my nose. I was scared for so long until I just put that together. Yo, that is ridiculous and hilarious. See, I have little light skin spots under my nose in both nostrils. That is why my relationship process slowed down. I was scared that my romantic life was ending, or so I thought, this drought was to end only for another to begin. Next time I see my doctor, I hope she will be able to provide me with an ointment for these little light patches. The only problem is that they are on my face, in the middle of my face. No one had it in them to let me know, but that is because they probably assumed I knew. Well, I'll get notice on my next appointment now.

One thing I thought about was the fact that girls tend to come in groups. Like there is never just one girl you talk to until you make it where there is that one girl you talk to. You finally think you found something, and then girls whom you never would have thought you would talk to start talking to you. Once I get things done and get my life figured out, I will dig into detail. It is just funny how this is coming to an end right after I think I figured out my main fault.

Another dilemma … my friends want me to drive to Hyde Park then Natick, and that really is not easy for me. I just have the feeling that there is another Brendan driving somewhere, and with my luck, I'm the one to meet him. That puts so much fear in me. I mean, I deal with it when I drive to work and stuff, but that is a reasonable route. I'm trying to get over it, and eventually I will, in a few years. Now saying that, let's hope as soon as I get over it, something else along those lines happens.

Life is coming to a climax, and it has looked pretty well so far. Now hopefully we go up, but we also may just take a dark toll and shoot up right after. That is usually how it goes. I'm gonna do as I tend to and make it as comfortable as possible. It is starting this way, but my mom is bringing up school again. A bright idea would be to just wait this suspension out and stay at Curry if this UMass Boston thing does not work out. Maybe I'll end up at some other UMass, but I just have to wait and make this as smooth as possible.

Easing into the new house, I like it. I just have to get used to driving in this area. You can't do that until you actually do it, but I'll wait until the weather breaks. For some reason, I just don't like driving in cold weather. When it is warm out, I am out more. Maybe because my accident was in the winter or just because when I am cold, I am so much more tense. I also like the way my car feels in the summer. Just gotta compromise somehow.

Life Will Try to Play You

See, life is really trying to play me. I thought I was heading up in the game in an intimate way, but nope, I'm still waiting. After I get my room together, we will see. Maybe I am being too impatient 'cause I feel like something is coming, and I'm just waiting for that. I believe that is why it is taking so long. I know I've made my mistakes, but damn, cut me some slack. I was in a whole-ass coma; I forgot some shit. Excuse my language, I am just sexually frustrated. That is a term I think is fit for my dilemma.

My life is depressing, but at the same time, I love it. Whenever I'm up, I can buy whatever I need when I need it, my blunts stay rolled, and even girls look as if they wanna link because they believe I can be played but let them rock. Once my room is situated and my money is settled and coming in steady, I think I'll be fine. That is what I have been waiting for. When I say settled, I mean in mass amounts and steady, just like the water. I'm trying to start hurricanes fictionally.

Another reason that accident means so much to me is because it was literally across the street from my house. That is ridiculous; who does that happen to? Give me some names, let me talk to them, and let me see how they felt. They have had to die or be in a two-month coma for me to relate to what happened. I really just don't like people telling me I didn't die like they were there, and it is a fact, like maybe not, but isn't it fair to say that a coma is temporary death at the end of the day? People say that every time you go to sleep, you could be with him, which may be true; so either way, I was with one person who means the most to me, God.

I am just scared of not doing what I want to do or being disappointed by not doing what I want to do or being the person I want to be. I also have the mindset to just get it done, so I believe it will get done. I did not think school would be this big of an obstacle, but it had to be something, right? With my luck, of course. I feel that when I'm done with this, I'm going somewhere, hopefully somewhere nice, and I won't stop until I get there. I need to get there, get somewhere at least.

Since I moved, my sleep has been marvelous. That is as much as I can say about this house. My room isn't painted, and none of my furniture is in, but I am just letting them do what they are doing for now. They've got a lot on their hands. My car has been dead for two days, and I am praying to God that the battery is not affected. Let my current problems diminish before you give me any more. I understand they are speeding up this process, but I can't keep having to stress as much as I have had too.

It's almost decision time; do I go back to Curry or go to UMass Boston? That all relies on if UMass Boston accepts me. They have to stop playing and just do it. I can take another problem after that; I'm reasonable. Like I know my second semester was not hitting as much as my first semester at Quincy College, but hopefully they will see the drop and know I was still dealing with problems related to that accident. I bring it up a lot, but that is just because it did just that much to me. If I could have drifted through that predicament, you would not hear as much about that accident from me.

I was told my room should be done by the end of this week, so that will be a good way to start the new year. Starting the year in a nice and new room signifies a fresh start. That could mean a lot or mean nothing at all, and I am trying to make the most of this. My car battery got charged up, so it is smooth-sailing again. I need to take it out somewhere tomorrow.

Focus on the things within your control. There is no point in sitting and feeling bad about something not going your way, especially if you cannot control it. Just find another way around that obstacle, and like I said, there are more ways than one. That's why I say if UMass doesn't go my way, I will just have to wait for Curry and take more precaution on campus this time around and see what I can do about a dorm. As I said before, I feel like it would make college so much easier.

If UMass does not work out next semester, then I am going to Quincy College for a semester just to get credits and keep my brain active. I should not take anything too strenuous, so I should not mind it, things like creative writing and what not. As of now, it sounds like a great idea, and I hope it stays that way throughout my whole time there again … it went well the first time. I feel like I am able to do one semester at Quincy, but then I have to be out.

If you think about it, look at how much I have to go through just for a simple-ass dorm. That dorm better be the dorm of my dreams when I get it. It should resemble exactly what I worked for. It could have been much simpler but I did it to myself, so I have to respect it, I guess. I know it will pay off soon; I just need that time to pick up the pace. I cannot wait until I can look back on the last couple of months not knowing where I would end up and say, "I made it."

This whole second time around has worked for me in the past; let's hope this time works like a charm, if not better. I get excited about it, but I am quick to calm myself down because I have had that feeling before. I feel like you have to go through all this if you did not go straight to a four year after high school. They make it harder for you. I think they were just like, "You can't fuck off for four years and go to a four year college." But nah, that was not the problem. They just don't want to see that.

CHAPTER 6

Let's Keep It Simple

One thing I always ask females is why something happened. If it is simple, I may get an answer; but I feel if I ask something in a deeper context, they would be afraid to say why. That may be because they don't want to seem like they think they are above or below anyone, and I really don't know why anyone would think that because I'm just as average as the next kid. I made as many slip ups as he did, and I may even have a good explanation for some of them. They may just not know and I'm overthinking, but if you saw what I saw, you would think the same way. Even if that's not the reason, there is a reason I do not know.

I can't say what I will be doing, but I have a better idea of how to do it. Keep God next to me and do what is called for to achieve my goals, and I think that is getting the required degrees. I could possibly get some connections in the job I hope to work at--- either a bank for connections or even TD Garden for bigger connections. I know how to get both of those jobs, and I believe I will get either of those jobs if I take the proper steps. I do not see anything tripping me up anywhere anytime soon. Let's hope I am right.

It is the new year, and my drought continues. Let's hope that is not a sign of how my year is about to be again. I just don't want that happening; I have suffered enough. I know I was not doing what I should have been doing, but I think God knows my punishment is up. School is about to start, so that will give me something to put my attention toward. Apparently, I am up for fall enrollment at UMass Boston and not spring, so I guess I'll go to Quincy College for a semester. I can do that; I have friends there. I'll just stay at my grandmother's whenever I have school.

My room is slowly coming together, and I am falling more and more in love with it. I got my TV and put posters up and half my clothes away. I went to my therapist today. It has seemed to help my driving anxiety, and I am thankful for that. I hope I have time for therapy when school starts. I should since I will most likely be at Quincy College for a Semester and at my grandmother's house during the week. That and going to therapy honestly might be best for me. I'll have to cross that commuting bridge when it comes. By that, I mean from UMass back to therapy every week. I mean, I will be home, but sometimes not with my car. I believe I can figure that out or my stress while driving will be gone hopefully. I could get so much done that way.

I went all the way to Lynn from Quincy and had a few interesting conversations. I have to get an actual job now, which I thought I had, but I have to work more days a week, and I will put my name down for more hours now. I just have to get my legs in shape. I was told to go on to Indeed, which is a job searching app to find better jobs, and I have found a few. I will look more into them tonight. Another conversation I found imperative is that weed is not for everyone, and I am thankful that I think it is suitable for me. There are people who smoke and get lazy or smoke to simply get things done. I am the type to either smoke and get things done or smoke, sit down for a while, and then begin to get things done. I don't think anyone understands that, but whoever does understand that needs to spread their knowledge to get people to accept it or perceive it suitably. Weed is really not for anything bad.

Life has seasons, and it looks like this one will suck. Only three days into the year but everything is starting to come into play. Once I get my schedule together for school, I think, if not hope, everything will come out positive. I am not stressed yet, but this is already taking a toll on my mental health. I have a life to live ahead of me full of this, and I have accepted it. I'm just trying to make my seasons as positive as possible.

It has been brought to my attention that people may also be a lot smarter than you think. I just thought everyone had basic knowledge a tad bit more or less, but I am in a new league with new people figuratively. Once again, I'm not in school anymore. I am trying to reenter college. I realized that a while ago, but it is time for me to switch gears in this atmosphere. I called Quincy College and set up a meeting with an adviser to pick my classes, and I will go to the office conducting FAFSA and have them get my money going to Quincy College. Hopefully I can get this done in a calm manner; not too much stress should be involved.

I am just not at the age to be able to think with my heart anymore. I am too nice to people; I give chances to people who will only take them and flip them. I have to think with my head. I mastered thinking with my heart; it is just the first thing I go to when things are just too complicated to figure out. Once I figure out how to properly think with my head, I will be fine. That usually does not happen until about thirty to forty but I am trying to get this all set and done way before then. Like I said, I aim to live a comfortable life and a complete lifetime.

It is about time for me to get over the anxiety I catch while driving. I really just don't have the energy to do that. I want to, but it is something that is just too hard for me to complete. No one understands how tight I grip the steering wheel when I drive and how sweaty my hands get under the most settled conditions. I just don't feel like I need that stress. I hope I can get by finding the rides I am finding until this phobia goes away. I take the car out--- it doesn't just sit there--- but only to places I need to be at by myself or I want to go by myself. I just HATE driving. I cannot extend that fact any more than I have. I think I am doing well as far as driving has gone. I can do better by going out places, but I just don't have the energy. I only drive to work and therapy if I have too. Over time it got better but I keep my focus behind the wheel.

I spoke to a publication consultant today, and I told him that I may be able to publish this in a few months after everything is done or when I can determine a way to end this. Hopefully I will know what school I will be attending after Quincy College so I can end this on a positive note. Once again, my life is starting to look up, and now I feel I am prepared to face anything. I am much wiser now socially, so I will be present when and where I need to be with people I am familiar with.

I am really just determined to graduate college now. Nothing else matters to me other than school and hopefully this TD Garden job. I will appreciate that dearly; my life will feel complete again. Everything will come together again smoothly, and I will try my best to hold it together. I said this last time, but once you think about it, I didn't really know much of anything. I was following signs, which is why I think I ended up there to learn what I learned, which I stated before.

There is this book called *The Hate You Give*, and I like the book and the way it is written. It is written similar to mine, and it talks about things similar to the way I discuss things and how they are going. I believe she also speaks about how she handled those situations, which is why I find the book relevant to mine. It also gives me more reason to write this book, seeing how far it is going. After speaking to the publisher and my therapist, I will just wait for a friend of mine to come edit it.

CHAPTER 7

These Girls

And back to these girls... I don't believe they know that I have been in this drought for two years. In other words, I haven't had sex in two years … at all. I keep hearing the word *thirsty* being thrown around toward me. I refuse to believe anybody will not be thirsty after a two year period, maybe more, of absolutely no sex. A drunk hookup was the best I could get. She didn't let me smash because she said God told her not to. That was dead-ass amazing. God might have the come-up about to come through, and you won't understand how great I am going to feel. I hope it happens sooner than later, maybe at its earliest. Moral of the story is, of course, I'm thirsty. I was thirsty last year. Now I am exhausted.

You know the mindset I had coming out of that hospital? My life could literally end in the blink of an eye, and I wouldn't expect it. I'm not even doing anything of that potential, but it is still a factor. I find that amazing. That amazingness dug me in the deepest hole imaginable. I was just looking for excuses to do the things I did, and I hate myself for that now in that aspect. I find it funny how when that aspect was up, my family issues were at its peak. But now I get no ass, and my family is just chilling, better than ever. I just need an occasional nut and a loyal girl, possibly with a car and who drives a lot, and she will be my number 1 obligation.

Another thing is my friends with parties and stuff. Shit is getting far, so we gotta use the highway. My uncle drives the same way, but this shit is insane. I do not understand how they do it. I just look up to God and hope he is watching over me dearly while I am out. This is so hard and stressful, but I feel I have to in order to be the average young adult I am. You know exactly what I'm talking about if you are an adolescent who goes out but not as much. This came out for discussion because I am going out tonight to Newton, which requires a highway … people really bug out on the highway. Thankfully, no one else does. I say that because imagine multiple people going down the highway doing at least eighty miles per hour. I only have to deal with one and have to be thankful for that because people will just think I am not fun to hang out with then I'll end up chilling with no one.

I thought cigarettes went out of style, but no, I was just with someone who hit the JUUL and smoked weed and cigarettes. That just made me think, *Why was she smoking those cigarettes or even that much?* She must be very stressed, and her story is probably just as stunning as mine but has no energy to write about it. I don't have much energy either, but all the energy I do have is used toward three places: this book, work, and school. It's the best way to use it smartly if you have as little energy as I do. And when I say run out of energy, I don't mean just stop and do something else but not do that task as well as you could have. I left the hospital prepared for this because my doctors informed me the first week I woke up that I would lack energy, either for a while or permanently. I do a fair amount now but require my rest, so it may be here but fading.

I had a talk with my mother today, and she said not to bring up the book or my accident in school now as if I bring it up all the time.

I wonder why she tells me not to speak of the book as much because I see that as networking or making people aware of something they will eventually be able to buy. I understand the reasons for the accident. People will try and take advantage of things I have since that accident, like my traumatic brain injury or my medical card. People have already taken advantage of the medical card factor, so I believe I'll be able to avoid that. It is just up to me to stay out of trouble and get my grades up. I can do that. I hope I can do that.

I've come to the conclusion that my name is hot-ass garbage in Quincy, my name with females anyway. I say that because after only a few nights of hanging out with Randolph people while living in Randolph, I already got girls who want dick. Maybe even one with a boyfriend, but I can't do that. I did my dirt, and I can't look back. I might fall. All I can say is we are rocking. I believe so anyway, In Quincy it will look like that every once in a while, and I'll get all excited and shit, then some shit pops off one way or the other. We're just gonna work. I think I have a team simply based on his words "gotta get you something nice" or something like that. Believe it or not, a girl said that, one with a boyfriend too.

Beautiful Dreams or Day-time

My beautiful dream feels as if it is starting, and it usually feels just like this. Now I don't know what to say because I said I was gonna stay on the right path last time, and I was so close, but look what happened. I'm gonna try this again and, as dumb as this sounds, stay away from the weed smokers, if you are away at school anyway. When I say that, I don't really know because people of all descents smoke weed, but I guess, pay close attention to small stuff like cleanliness. "Dirty dorm, dirty dude"---guess I have to go by that now. I really do not know how to go about this college thing after Quincy College; it is easy for some and difficult for others.

After a while, it came to me that I tend to just smoke to cope with the feelings I have because I know if they were bad, I would just think of ways to do things to people who have done me wrong. I guess it is another reason to smoke if that does not go along with anxiety and depression. It helps me confide my feelings into this book. Of course, I may have some times where I seem tense, and that is most likely because I am in the middle of that task or just got done doing that particular thing--- like when I was talking about going out with my friends and them having to take the highway. Whenever you see me cursing, that is most likely why.

Now I know that anytime I experience pain or anything bad in my life, all I can do is laugh because it happened to me, depending on the situation. I say this because today I tried to assist my stepdad taking the futon meant for downstairs off the truck, and when he pulled the box, he fell back. I had my slippers on, and I was right behind him. He had steel-toed boots on, and he stepped on my foot then dragged it. All I could do was laugh because I thought about it right before it happened like, "lemme go put some shoes on," but they were pulling up, so I was like, "Nah, lemme not prolong the situation," then some shit like that happened. I found it hilarious, still do.

I find it funny how you can live a completely different life from others and people still expect you to conduct your life just as normal as them. I went from getting ass at least three times a week, I kept count, to not getting ass in TWO YEARS. My god. I think I lost count, and that's ridiculous. I think I feel it coming once again, and let's hope I am not lying to myself. I feel like Tom Brady with a team behind me, so I feel unstoppable. Turns out that team was just a drill squad preparing me for god knows what.

I had a talk with my uncle--- his name is Shane--- and he told me that everything becomes a grind, and I didn't know what that meant. I hope everything I love to do does not become a task. I feel like most things will, but not everything. I am trying to get a job I love, so that way, I am doing something I love every day. He also told me I am too friendly, and I think I have learned that, but he says I still move the same way. I thought I was, and I still think I am. He said that because I smoked a blunt with the people who helped us move in; I didn't invite them in for dinner. I believe I can say I have learned and am continuing to learn. Hopefully that phase is done with. I learned; if you're gonna test me and I will have to pass. I believe I am gonna pass by just keeping my space with people and getting my work done. I am gonna practice that at Quincy College. I'm still gonna smoke with my friends, but I can't do those 3:00 a.m nights anymore or not as much depending on the plans.

Common Sense

Apparently, my uncle gotta teach me the game all over again. That is because I didn't have a smooth transition into adulthood. When I say that, I mean I just forgot how it goes, and maybe there are some new rules. Some stuff may just have gone out of style but will come back soon. Like he said, "you can't chase a female with your personality. Let them chase you. They have already made their decision after your social media at the end of the day. That is after school is done for you.: I am surprised my friends weren't the ones to do that. Maybe they thought I was chillin' because I am. I mean, I don't think it's the end of the world; but I mean, damn, two years is a long time. After hearing that, I thought about it, and I was about to have a girl come over and run through it because that would be a nut from true desperation whether I like it or not. I will just have to see what happens next.

That talk also made me a lot more determined to get this degree due to him saying, "everything is a grind." He's going back to school for a degree now anyway. He said it was reckless to move out of state at his age with no degree. I don't believe I am moving out of state, but it's still a good reason to get one. I think like this every time I'm home and things change at school just because other people my age changed my mind, but nah, I learned, and it's early.

By the way, if there were actual police at Curry College, they would have believed that was not my bag at all, and that pisses me off because they really did not have the common sense to believe that bag was not mine. I feel like anyone with a little bit of common sense and who knew the value of weed would say, "I'm sure you would not leave with thirty grams with unsupervised" but then again, they didn't know me as a person, so why would they think that ? I have to put my head down and grind this out. I just have to look at this as if I'm going away to school. I Should make this simple. It's all about how you look at things.

I feel like when I was in a coma, everyone got together or there was a big social media epidemic about me. Obviously, there were some Instagram pictures, but all girls are acting differently toward me. Well, that is how things go in Quincy. It seems like they all know something I don't or they all know something I don't know they know. Everything has two ways they can go, but I can't find a way to go about figuring it out properly, so I don't do it.

Another thing on my mind is that I should start to show more emotion so people could see my feelings. I really just don't care unless it affects me, then that particular task gets done. Even though I get what I want or need, it may be easier to get that thing. Just showing that you want something while trying may lead to success. And now whenever I get a thought to put in the book, I just have to get up and write it. It doesn't matter if it is three in the afternoon or two in the morning. I get the best ideas in bed at night, but I am damn near sleep, so I try to remember that note then try to go into detail based on that note. It works SOMETIMES; I do not have time for other times.

Okay, now my mom would like me to keep Lids while working for TD Garden. That would be two jobs. But I have the opportunity to land a job at a bank in North Quincy as security along with TD Garden, and that would also be two jobs plus Lids if I want it. My mom says to keep Lids since they stuck with me. I could respect that decision; I'm just gonna be juggling school too. If everything goes as planned, I'll be at Quincy College with the occasional commute to TD Garden or Lids. The bank is my last choice and is only a choice because a former teammate works there. I just hope she realizes that either way this goes, I'm juggling multiple jobs and school.

Also, I will need my uncle Shane to stop saying, "You have an answer for everything" because I am not 100 percent positive, but I am pretty sure every statement requires an answer to reassure you of my opinion. I know I have an answer for everything, and that leads to intense conversation that I may write about. I just need him to put some thought into my answers. Maybe they will positively alter his mindset. He thinks he is 1,000 percent right compared to me because of his age and stories, but I have just as dramatic stories. I just have different causes and different people. He has the worst portrayal of everything this world has to offer like every other middle-aged man; I hope I am not forced to think that way or even want to.

Something that has been on my mind is that I really don't want the aspect of life my uncle has or the story he had to learn it from.

I do not know his story, but I know whatever he did was on his record until he got it sealed. One thing he said to me and stuck with me was,"People judge you off the character you carry in certain situations." I think I handle situations well, and I hope I can handle all situations just the way I did after work a couple nights ago. My car was dead and my phone was dead, but I just thought through it carefully, and everything went as planned. I was proud of that. I just have to remember to stay calm and carefully think of ways to resolve that problem. My uncle said I was also portraying a hoodlum when I wore my do-rag, and that may be true, but I am just trying to get my waves started. They may have started the do-rag trend, but I am changing it. I may be bugging, but I am pretty sure the average black person has their waves or they are absorbing the nappy look like I used to, nappy Afro with a fade.

He says my retail references mean the most so I should iron my pants and not enter smelling like weed. And I can understand that, but I like to let my work speak for me. Everything gets done, and all customers I deal with leave with a smile, so no one has a reason to give a bad reference. I like my managers, and my managers like me. I played Youth Football with one, so I am not stressed, and let's hope that just because he said that people won't start giving bad references or only bring up the fact that I smell like weed. Like I am not bugging; I'm young, and my job gets done when asked to. Me being young should explain the weed. I'm not gonna be a thirty-five year old man in my job smelling like weed unless I just happen to be owning a dispensary, and my job getting done should make the weed smell irrelevant, but nah, he said none of that matters. It is the facts you have, and right now, I am trying to get my facts straight. Facts as in documentation. I believe I can, so I will.

CHAPTER 8

My Name Means Something

People look at my last name and automatically know I have a long story. Going back to the beginning of time, I really have no clue how to explain the start of my last name so I won't even make an attempt. It is a lot to carry, but I believe I can make a good representation of that last name and my family. Being able to do that in the manner I do seems simple, but there is some hardship along the way. I feel as if I am a resilient person who tries not to let things too minor get in the way of my task at hand, but sometimes the situation may become too big to handle. I just have to keep a smile on my face because they are just growing pains, and I have to go through them in order to mentally grow.

I think my uncle expects me to be mad at the people involved or the fact that I have had to deal with this based on the way he portrays people. What they will get will come, and I will get where I am going. I'll see how I'm feeling when I'm there. He doesn't seem racist, but his anger gets the best of his words. I believe me not having any hatred or resentment toward them makes it that much better, and I'll just have reasons to believe blessings will come, and that will push me to work toward them. All I can do now is to do my work well and hope.

Every time I go out with uncle Shane, we have very interesting conversations that I want to take note of in my book, but I am just too focused on the road to even look at my phone. So if I am lucky, I will remember that conversation to note later, or sometimes I'll feel comfortable, but only if I have other places to place my focus on--- like sometimes we are driving through Boston and I like to look out the window and we are cruising slowly so I can multitask.

I like going out, but sometimes he has a very bad outlook on certain subjects, so I just get upset but do not want to argue because he is driving and already driving fast at times. I can only imagine how he drives when angry.

One thing I did think about while lying in bed last night is that I and Shane have the same mindset in some aspects, but in other aspects, he is very one-minded. I believe he has hate from past experiences still invested into him. Like for school, he recently got the mindset to get it out of the way as fast as possible, which he should have been doing since my age but I guess stuff had to happen and he had things to realize. I think he has the worst perspective of people and the way life goes based on the time he started to take life seriously. He didn't spend his twenties like me in college or trying to go to college, but he is almost forty and all he wants is his degree now. He also judges people without knowing them. Like he said I was with someone with goth attire on, and based on the face he made after stating that, he was not too fond of it I don't tend to put my attention toward people wearing goth attire, but if one approached me, I am not going to shy away from him or her; I'll just learn about them and their story.

CHAPTER 9

Sleep Struggles

I just read something that said, "Everyone struggles with sleep because sleep requires peace." It made sense to me because you do need peace to get sleep. I can prove that because my sleep was terrible at the old house because I almost died across the street. I just needed peace of mind. I can't say I fall straight to sleep now; I just plan how my day will go tomorrow. That makes a lot of things simpler, and that makes me proud. I just need to peacefully sit and think about my moves before I make them, and I go to bed whenever I get that time, which is also when I come up with ideas for my book but too tired to take note of them.

Okay, so Shane gave me sixty dollars cash one day and told me I was going to spend fifty-four. He also called the store to see if I could get a discount. He said I wasn't getting a particular discount. I got to the store, and the first question I asked when I got there was, Will I have a chance to receive any discounts? And with no questions asked, he gave me a business card with a bunch of deals on them. I ended up spending forty bucks and saving twenty; the price came up to thirty-eight dollars or something like that. I got like a dollar and some change back.

When I went back to the car, he asked how much change I got back. I said one dollar and some change then showed him the receipt then proceeded to give him the money. I was gonna keep the twenty because he'd never really ask for change and I thought it wouldn't be a big deal. Then he jumped to the conclusion that I needed his money or tried to take it, but in reality, I just took a situation he gave me and made it better for me. It pissed me off that he thought I'd want anything from him, and he didn't like that because he told my grandma. And I didn't like it either because he tried to call me a fuckboy, like I had time to hear that, so I told my mom. It was not a mistake; it was not like I hid the receipt from him or told him no when he asked for the money because that'd be a fuckboy thing to do. But if that was the way he wanted to view me, then Imma let him do that. I got things I am trying to have fall in place.

Keep Dreaming

I have times when I feel like something great will happen and I will be someone important somewhere, maybe everywhere, but then I have times when I start to think about everything crumbling and I hope and pray that does not happen. I just want to get up and stay up. I think I took the majority of a life span in Ls in that accident. It should cover my adulthood, maybe even most of my adulthood. That accident took away my senior year of high school. I do not know if that is a bad thing or a blessing. It also took away some very great memories; man, I want those. My life was deadass a movie.

Something changed about me after that accident. I know this because there is no way I went from having threesomes to not getting anything in two years. Once I find that out, something will happen, and I will figure it out. I will ask my friends tonight, one who is a girl, and let's see what they say. Fact of the matter is, they are the ones I had a threesome with. That is how I know I will get a true answer.

I will say, if I could do a few things in my life over again, I certainly would. I can't lie, but I don't know how my life will turn out or if I would be thankful about it. I say this because I just thought about a time my friend Will took me to one of his Saint Sebastian's parties. That is a private school in Needham. Their parties tend to be a good environment, nothing crazy. But one of their friends picked me up and was like, "Ayo, it's Kijuan," and I was like, "Nah, cool it." But honestly, no one knew me …..I should have done something. I do not know. I mean, I can't care now, but it just ran across my mind' like it can just do that. The Same thing happened at my graduation. They called my name, and I just sped across the stage because I shy away from attention immediately. I didn't run across the stage, but I walked at a fast pace. If I could do that again, I would do that too. I'm gonna stop doing that because I want that to be an occasion.

I just figured out why my mom always assumes something happens to my friends after a certain amount of time of not seeing them. I say that because me and Shane were going out as much as my friends were going out, and after a few times of going out with Shane, I guess he found a reason to not trust me. I do not get it. I answered his question; he asked how much change, not how much I left the store with. I just have to let him go through his emotions and deal with that on his own.

Quincy College is going well once again. I just have to figure out how I am gonna make it through this English class. I have a plan, so hopefully this goes smoothly. I am just gonna go sit next to this person in my class whom I think knows what he is doing. Well, he seems like a cool, even-minded person; we can help each other pass this class. I know God has a plan for me, and I think I see it and hope I complete it. I'm spending one more semester here in hopes to transfer to UMass Boston where someone I liked a while ago may transfer with me; let's see what happens after that. I've been telling her about all the things I have got to do, like going on the red carpet at the SAG-AFTRA at Laugh town next to Westin for my extra role in a Netflix special, or we just talk about what I did at Curry College. She has a boyfriend now, but I feel something happening with that. I don't wish for anything to happen, but if it does, then I gotta let it rock, I guess.

Something particular about therapy is that it has made me more content with the way things go in life. Most of the things go positive, but when things don't go as planned, I can just take an L in stride. I used to spend time thinking about it, but once those words are out, they are out. I spent some more time thinking about that accident though, and it took me a while, but the only reason I feel so traumatized is because I do not remember it. I went on that road the other day, and it was so smooth. Like how did that happen? Something will happen that leads to me forgetting that accident even happened. I just cannot wait.

Crazy that I'm already lit for my thirties and I am just getting into my twenties. I just have a feeling something big is happening. I do not know what, but I'm just going to cruise into this and keep a positive mindset and help where I can or feel the need to. I just hope I'm not fooling myself, but I mean, I was just on the red carpet. That gotta mean something. That is probably why the girl I saw on set was there like a damn model. I heard her though; you gotta look the part. Now that I think about it, I did; I looked approachable. I met someone there by the name of Peter. He's a cool dude. He said he was a filmmaker, so I assume he's on his way up in that business, and hopefully I'm right there with him. He introduced me to one of his higher-ups. His name is Joe, and he looked like a very important person, so let's see where that goes.

I cannot get over the fact that I had the life to live at Curry College until that happened. I had everything except a dorm. My wallet had a tendency of being thick, and that was different considering I was in college, so I was supposed to be broke. The way money was coming in, I considered myself broke and rarely spent money on campus. I was upset when I had to spend a dollar to get some ice cream. I was mad because NOBODY else had to pay, but they also had dorms, so I couldn't be too mad.

CHAPTER 10

Twenty-one!

My twenty-first birthday is coming up, and that just means I have decisions to make and things to do. That comes at a strange time because school is starting. I would have to go get a new license, and I want to go somewhere. I Might just end up in Boston, but I wanted to go to Vegas because my brother had brought it up in a phone call one day and said he has a friend with a penthouse over there. I wanted my money to be up for that, and it shouldn't be a problem, but once again, let's hope.

I spoke with my therapist and realized I was thinking too far ahead. I was trying to release a movie based on this book before I even finished the book. It just tells you where I think this book will go and what this book will do. You just have to get one thing complete at a time; think ahead but don't think too far ahead. Once I get the book published, then maybe there will be talks of releasing a movie.

Now that I am thinking about it, you know that girl I said was transferring with me to UMass Boston? Turns out that is a dub; she is not going. I just got caught up thinking too far ahead. That leads me to say that I am still in this drought, the drought I thought was ending a little while ago. That leads me to say this: my expectations for thirty have tripled considering there is a 3 in the number 30.

Highs and Lows

I saw a tweet on Twitter that said, "People really are thinking their life is over. Ridiculous" or something like that. I needed to see that tweet. It just reassured me that it is not just me. Same thing with that drought, my friend told me he's been in this dilemma for a year and a half. Another friend said four months, but he looked like he was exhausted for the meanest minute. I recently saw another tweet saying, "I will be an author by the summer." That got me excited because I'm writing a book, and an author writing books most likely gets published, and I am aiming for a published book by the summer.

The thing is, sometimes I feel like everything is coming together well and sometimes I feel like things are falling apart or probably literally falling apart. Most of the time, I will be able to handle it, but sometimes it takes a toll on me, and it just sits in the back of my head and comes up whenever I have the time to sit and think--- especially when I am in bed and have literally everything running through my mind. At times I dislike it, but sometimes it is wonderful. I try to keep good thoughts, but that gets difficult.

So someone I call my brother just called me and explained what he has been going through the past few weeks. He has been sleeping in his car with a pregnant wife--- the wife he married after getting out of jail. Speaking of that, he has another case, but it's open. He says he has literally no one to handle this with. The only reason he is not here right now is because he is in Georgia. That is my brother, someone I care about extremely, and hearing that gave me so much stress. I thought my life was getting obscure, but no, I do not think I knew how to take the things I've gone through. But I feel like I took them on the chin.

I learned something last night: you can either be on girls' back and they can call you a creep or straight up mind your business and girls will think you're gay. I learned this because a girl whom I didn't even speak to while I was at Currycalled me randomly, and she asked me if I was gay. She was cool and all, but damn, that is my name at that school, I guess. I am glad I left. After I told her about all the reasons I have for acting the way I acted, she wanted to switch up and said she felt like a dick. It's cool though; I just have to talk more. When I was at Curry, I didn't know any of them and I was a commuter, so it made it that much harder to properly socialize. Once again, I could have formed my own friend group if I had a dorm. That happened because people don't ask questions; I guess it was a secret to know my sexual orientation. And no one bothered to ask, "Why is your eye like that?" but she did. Maybe because it sounds disrespectful or maybe it's the scar or my quiet manner.

People have to start speaking more. My uncle believes people have bad communication skills, and that's it. People are not dead-ass mute, but if you have something to tell me, just say it. Do not just assume that I will pick up the hint. Everyone does not think the same, and if I ask, do not get annoyed. It is a question; answer it and carry on. I do not know if this is a game I will just have to play until maybe mid-twenties or if this is something I am about to learn going throughout life, hopefully early in life.

I literally can't hold shit. That's depressing. Every time I get up, that shit falls, and it goes from all to nothing. The thickness of my wallet when I went to Curry had to go down with fees and food, and shit like that, but I mean, I guess that's fine. I just got a $600 deposit to my wallet, so that was nice. I got a gold chain, might get another or a jersey. We are gonna see about that. The amount of ass I was receiving--- I think it was too much. That is the only reason I think I am suffering this terribly. I'm holding this job I barely work at, but I hope I can hold my next actual job. I will be on the move; just let me know and I will be there. Now if or when I get back up and start having sex again, I'll be damned if something happens and you find me back in these slums, just know that.

The Other Problem

I told my mom about my problem of me not being able to get any ass or, as she says, leg. I had to, but it's not like I just bust out with it. She came into my room and was like, "Give me two problems you have right now." I tried to avoid the question, but she came in and sat down like she was about to be there for a minute. And I just said, "Okay, I have one problem I cannot find the solution to, and it is the fact that I have not had sex in two years." She sat back and thought about it, and I could see in her face that everything started adding up. I do not know how to feel about that decision, but that is literally the only problem at the moment. My money is where I need it to be, and I'm in school. I believe I am doing well, thank God, and I know life fluctuates, but I have a deep pit to crawl out of.

People are just scared to ask one question. I know this, and I'm taking it to the grave 'cause I was finessed. I woke up from a damn coma, and two days later, somebody texted me talking crazy. And I was about to experiment, but I couldn't bring myself to do that. If someone would have asked, I would have had the best explanation possible; they'll know soon. God will put me together in front of all of them. They should know who they are when it happens.

I asked some people what changed about me, and they said nothing, maybe a little ruder. I would say "Suck my dick" but that would be rude of me. Before this, some of the girls were giving me ass. In other words, they were on backs, and it was simple to have sex with them. Now there is no one, but I have to keep in mind I am twenty and I am not the only one who is going through this. God will put me together in front of all of them.

People are always talking about,"Oh, Imma teach you" but no one is teaching me something that I clearly forgot. I just need to relearn my ways with girls. People see it, but they just don't wanna say it for some reason. It is mind-blowing to me to be completely honest, and sometimes it is scary, one or the other. I do not know what I'll do if years from now something happens and I get u and someone says, "Remember your twenties? This is why." They won't, but damn, that would be hilarious.

I am a very different kid, and that just stood out to me a lot more than usual because I just thought of all the things I have to do tomorrow--- which is going to school, going to the gym, then going to work--- and I just began to applaud myself in excitement for it, saying, "There you go, Kijuan. That's what I like to see." I don't think I was doing that in high school because there are some pictures that tell me all I need to know about high school. My life was top 5 high school experiences; I was rocking with my teachers and my classmates or teammates. I enjoyed going to school. Of course, it had to be all early; but other than that and the occasional test, I was chilling. The parties were a different story, and we can't start the conversation about me and women back in the day mainly because I do not remember.

I can tell you about a few that I remember, and this one I find ridiculous. I think she tried to set me up; We will talk about that later. But I ran a train, something I still can't believe I did. And I was friends with that girl again when I moved to Randolph. Me, the girl I had it with, and my friend Eric were all friends after. I haven't spoken to her recently, so I'm not gonna put her name out there. I really do not know what happened to her; she just faded. She might pull up, again one day, but who knows. I don't really know or remember many other stories, but the keyword is *many*. I only remember some really different experiences. If I cannot remember it, it is not valid. I really only remember my girlfriend because she was the only one who meant something to me.

If I could trade anything for high school just to do it over again, I do not know if I would want to or not--- just because of the closeness I feel that I have with God himself now. I spent a good amount of time with him for a short visit. If none of that ever happened, I think no one understands what would have happened. I don't even know, to be honest with you. This book probably would have never been written because my life wouldn't be as interesting as it is. I would most definitely be in school about to be done and maybe even playing lacrosse. I really hate Brendan thinking about it, but we're here; he tried it.

I would still be in school because I would not have had a marijuana license or a medical card, as you may call it. I would have had no reason for him to say it was mine. Who says I would have even been with him? I might have been at a whole-ass other school. I might have been playing lacrosse, so I probably wouldn't be able to smoke as much as I do now. Maybe every now and then--- MAYBE. Still no clue what my major would have been, maybe psychology, maybe took a whole other route. I really believe it'd be psychology because I am still doing it and I don't remember sports much--- just pictures, trophies, lacrosse sticks, and friends and only a couple of all of those things left. I've got one friend from lacrosse who is really my brother because we also played football together and went to middle school together. He is in the military right now, so I hope he is staying up over there. He just left California for North Carolina, I'm pretty sure--- maybe South Carolina, but I'll find out. I've got a few other team-mates where it is all love when I see them. One dates my ex, and shit happens, so I gotta let that rock.

Someone recently brought up the idea of laser eye surgery to help with the miscorrelation in my eyes. That option was given to me in the hospital, but the last thing I need is to have to go through this world blind. This world will play the fuck out of me if that happened. I can tell now, I'm as fine as I possibly could be, and people still try to take advantage of one thing or the other. I mean, get your bread but pick your poison.

If you have a dream, do your best to make that dream come true and don't let anyone tell you that dream won't come true. You are doing that for a good reason. "If you wanna kill a dream, tell it to a small-minded person." That means you just can't talk about those things with people who cannot see what you see. Make them see it; maybe they will help you. If they want to help you, keep them in or around your life just because they show that they really care about you and your future. Know the difference between someone who cares about you for your features and someone who is around for your future. That will help a lot when the time comes.

Something told me that I didn't push some people away but God removed them, and when I say something, it is this app called Sprinkle of Jesus. It gave me a lot of faith in God's plan and what he is doing. I say that because whatever he is doing is going into effect. That lets me know he is paying attention to me and anyone else paying attention to him. Speaking of his plan, I need to find the number that called me asking me about getting my book published. I was just looking and ended up calling some office building somewhere. I had absolutely no influence in getting a book published. I should have saved it, but I gave them a certain month to call me back, which was either March or May--- something with an *M*. I just gotta keep that in my prayers and keep doing what I do.

False Alarm

The woman I was about to try and give some dick to is pregnant ...how? Please let me know. Oh yea she was hoein' and that shit caught up, creeped up. She is stressing, so I don't know what to say. I refuse to be a stepfather, so it's looking slow as hell on her now, but I mean, it could have been. All I told her was, "You gotta want the baby"--- just because I see enough unwanted babies. I do not know if that is because I watch too many movies or this is real life. Now that I think about it, as seldom as I see one, I shouldn't see any.

I think I figured out why I am in this drought. I deserve it. I cheated on a girl who was there for me, but I had the mind that I could die at any time, so whenI went out, I was going out with a bang. I wanted people to be like, "Man, that Kijuan---boy, he did his thing with the ladies." I wanted people to speak great in some way on my name, and I made sure at all times in my life I was doing something where people can speak proudly of me, like when I played football. People give credit where it is due till this day. I didn't just figure that out, but it was just what reassured me when a girl said she was not into me and said she saw me as a friend, and I haven't seen her since like junior year of high school. If you think I'm ugly, keep it a bean and say that. Say what you feel. I know she was lying, and that is what pissed me off. But you just have to brush it off; it shouldn't hurt you. Keep going.

I'm one step closer to where I would like to be. I went to Summer Street in Boston for the third time, but this time I went to go do my background check and fit my uniform. I will get my uniform during my orientation, hopefully next week--- maybe two weeks. Once I get this job, I may try for an apartment in Quincy to make my commute to Boston easier since I will potentially spend a lot of time on that commute. The only problem with that is how expensive that will be. I just have to have faith in myself to make things connect. It will be up to me for this to go smoothly. I'm still thinking about that.

The crazy part about today was that the lady whom I signed working papers with had a daughter who went to Curry. She died at Curry. What does that mean? I don't know, but it meant something with me toward Curry. I don't know if I want to find out. My coworker told me that Curry used to be a mental asylum. Now that he said that, I can totally see it. It makes perfect sense. Now I just wonder why no one told me about their history before making my decision, not a few months after I'm banned.

So I lost my license; this week was going so well too. Everything was getting done smoothly--- No mishaps. I thought I crossed the finish line, but nope. Another example of why you can't think that until you are done. I don't know how to feel about this since most of the things I have had to do have gone smoothly, but then the fact that I lost my wallet is heartbreaking honestly. I'm mad because that person didn't say anything, and I'm disappointed because I didn't hear it fall out and I didn't make sure I had all the things I needed before I left. Life has been going pretty smooth lately, so I really don't know how to feel. I can't have this happening all the time, so my alertness for my wallet is about to shoot right back up. I remember I thought this happened last year, but no, my high school had it because someone attempted to take it but failed then dropped it, so I guess he succeeded, depending on his intentions.

I've been blessed lately, so a blessing may come after this, and I feel I am in a good place to start. Mike also said that, which gave me hope. Mike is my stepfather, if I haven't said that. My mom also asked when I was moving out, and my therapist said the average age was twenty-six so I will aim for twenty-four, possibly sooner, hopefully. This is weird because I feel lighter now. Maybe that person needed that, and that is why the person didn't say anything. I have an idea who it was, but I do not know her. And I'm not 100 percent positive, so let me not assume.

CHAPTER 11

Guess I'm from the Hood

I just thought about it because it has been brought up lately, but kids at Curry really call Quincy the Hood. I do not believe that at all, but I mean, no one was trying anything with me. And when they did some shit, they got me banned from campus. I want to go up there, but only they know what they will do with me if I go over there. I think it is trespassing if I go on that campus, so that is awfully slow for me. And when I say that, I mean I could go to jail or they could just try to fine me for something else. And they have been chilling on the other things they fined me for, so I'm chilling and minding my own business even though that is my business, which is the ridiculous part.

Sometimes I hop in my feelings and start thinking about the things I can't remember I did wrong but know I did wrong. When I say that, I mean the things I did in my relationship. I vow to never do that again. I didn't know who I was, and that should be clear if they know about the gay dude. But Imma brush it off because when I am up, I'm up. I keep saying I won't let things fall, but something always happens, one thing if not the other. But I will be damned if I do not try my absolute hardest when I start getting what I need frequently.

I have to start teaching communication skills because I'm at AAA. I was sitting with some guy on one side and my grandmother on the other. I asked the man simple questions, like what a question on the sheet meant and when his name would be calle, but Nana tapped me and told me to stop talking to people like I was in the wrong for asking simple questions. I can understand that because she is from a generation or era of being seen and not heard, so I have to respect it but bring her out of it steadily; she is almost there.

Okay, so now Curry College's black students are getting death messages or something like that. I can't tolerate that, so maybe this whole situation will be best for the hand I was dealt. That is a coincidence because I just found out about a death in the college right after realizing Curry used to be a mental asylum. How come absolutely no one told me about any of this? They just said, "Oh, really," smiled, and shook their heads when I told them I was going there. That is what I mean when I say people need to work on their communication skills. Speak on what you feel or know, right or wrong, because that may start a discussion. The fact that people from that school are calling Quincy the hood is beyond me. They have people dying over there on a predominantly white campus--- may even have a higher death rate than Quincy.

The girl I planned to have sex with had a miscarriage. Now I am not proud of that, but it shows that God had certain intentions for her--- Not with me but for life in general. I might just happen to be in those plans. That would be nice, but that is not my main concern. I only care to know if she was straight with that situation. She said she was stressed, but soon after, I saw her tweet something about God and maybe his plan, so hopefully she is going the right way about this whole situation.

I will most likely be doing a podcast my friend I played football with is starting, and that is a way for me to publicize what I am doing, and the way I think makes me feel everyone has the worst perception of me. God told Mario to do this for things like that. It's a great idea; I may start doing that with him. Because he may be successful with that and do something with it. So saying that, a book and a whole-ass podcast--- no one can say, "Oh, I didn't know" or just act ignorant toward that fact. The movie would only make that statement truer; I hope that happens.

People did not take notice of the fact that people could literally tell me I did anything before that accident and I had to believe them. Some of it was unbelievable, but the other three-quarters of it was in question 'cause I really did not know who I was. I didn't know if I was gay, straight, a bad person, an angel, anything. It has been two years, and no one realized it, so they probably won't. It's okay because something will happen, and I'm just waiting and working. I have to keep a humble mindset regardless of what happens. If nothing happens, on to the next thing, whatever that is.

By the end of this book, you should have a better understanding of how to stay focused; and this book shows you that if I can do it, you can regardless of your situation. I was in a two-month coma, and now I'm here--- of course, with some scars and bumps in the road, but I'll get some Band-Aids in heaven. There might not even be any scars when I get up there. After that two-month coma, I get suspended and banned from college …me, for doing absolutely nothing. But that has been working out accordingly, and I hope it continues to do that. Now while dealing with those things, I had minor issues that I mentioned throughout the book, but I get through those too, and I hope to get through this little drought I'm in.

People always relate me to Curtis Jackson. You may know him as 50 Cent, but I know him as a businessman. Some people say it is because of the do-rag, and some say the tank top, but if you look at him now, he is not wearing any of those things. He typically looks presentable in interviews I have seen him in. He looks like a businessman or simply an important person. He is someone I am aspiring to be, and I think it is meant for me to meet him because he has a television series where there is a character who looks exactly like me. I found it funny, and all I said when I saw it was, "Why couldn't you hit me up 50?" And my mom used to have pictures of him and stuff.

After looking into my eye dilemma, trying to figure out the miscorrelation in my eyes, I came down to the conclusion that I have optic nerve damage or diplopia. I hope it is diplopia because optic nerve damage is irreversible. I don't have time for it; I have some things I need to do that advise for two eyes to correlate. I did some more research and found out I had binocular diplopia, which is caused by many things like strokes and is most common. I said stroke specifically because it is damaging to the brain.

I know this is a joke now. I was just on Snapchat and saw some girl I think I knew smoking a blunt on a bed in her dorm. And she was nowhere near a damn door or window--- without a care in the world. Yet I get banned because someone SAID I had weed and brass knuckles on campus when I wasn't even on campus, might I add. That leads me to think this is all just a game to test my patience, so when I get there, I'm chilling.

Also by the end of this book, I expect anyone who knew me before and after that accident to understand what I was going through personally. No one could or no one tried to help with anything I was dealing with. I just had empty promises out the ass. It took me two years or maybe more to relearn everything, but lately I have felt more of an original Kijuan---Simply based on the way he talked or texted. I've been proud of it, and I hope he will be here when I begin to experience all my blessings to come. I strongly believe he deserves that experience most.

One thing I will not do is act like all my friends had empty promises. We have some honorable mentions like Sammy, Will, Fitzy, and a few others. I remember them specifically because I can see them talking to me about something like that. If they said they would do it, they did it. I really appreciate them and this girl named Carolyn who was there for me when I woke up---Seemed like every day. Of course, I tried my thing a little later on, but she said that she looked at me like a brother, maybe the same way half these other girls feel. And that is awfully ridiculous; I'm not that damn friendly. I really rocked with her, and I felt like we could do something, but that's slow, so I can't let that get me down. I just gotta find something better to fill that void.

Another half of my friends think that I am Kanye West or think that I relate to him, but I don't know how to feel about that. I'm pretty sure he is hated in the U.S, but I saw a video on Twitter of him in Africa having the time of his life. The point is, he is rocking globally. I don't believe people know or see that because I know for a fact that I did not think the majority of black people hating him in one country would lead to a country full of black people loving him. One thing I don't see is Kanye having his slavery mindset over there. He either doesn't talk about it or they like the concept. I personally don't think slavery was a choice, and I hope he soon realized that after saying it. I have yet to figure out why they think I relate to Kanye, possibly because of my view on some things, things he hasn't even expressed. I really do not know; I just have to make the best of it.

Empty Promises

After getting those words out about my friends, it took a little while of thought, but I soon realized that those empty promises may just be the real world. That is my reality check, so that is why I consider some friends close friends. They keep me at bay. Like I have one friend named Jeff, Haitian dude, who stays tryna finesse me, but I got a couple friends on that note. I just hate when he does it, because I think he thinks he's really that slick. Now that doesn't mean people go around finessing me. My brain is always on the go. It's maybe a little sluggish at times, but it's going, and it catches up.

Honestly, getting banned from college was not circumstantial for me because I really didn't do anything. I was two hours away doing a movie for Netflix. I don't think many people should know that because sadly people will have a certain resentment toward me for that, and I mentioned the fact that I was not there doing that in my meeting with the people at Curry, which is why I think I ended up being suspended, which eventually caused me to be banned. If you ask me how any of that works, I really can't tell you, but it was a blessing because Curry is expensive. I probably shouldn't have been there, but something told me to stick it out. I don't know who it was or where it came from, but I stuck through it for the most part or any party to be honest.

It is still crazy to me how fast my life went from relatively good to that bad in a few seconds. It just goes to show how fast life can turn on you. That is why I learned to never get too comfortable. I can't wait for a time where I can just sit back and relax without a care in the world in a house I can call mine. But until then, I will keep a chip on my shoulder. That helps me get what I need to be done and on time.

All I need is time and the proper utensils, and it will get done. I have that much faith in myself.

The last few years have had some very valuable lessons. When you reach eighteen, you will begin to see people for who they truly are, for better or for worse. I say that because some lessons have been taught that I may have just forgotten but do not personally believe I ever encountered. They were good and well-timed because they were early. The problem now is that I have the tendency of seeing the better in everyone, which could only be true for some people.

So now I will work at Lids---as seldom as I do--- go to school, and work at TD Garden. That means I am just gonna be on the go non-stop, but that also means my money should look marvelous. I should not have to stress about any bills or deadlines anytime soon. Doing all these things make me want to make that go smoothly and find a schedule. Once I get the days figured out, I should be fine. Like I expected I will be spending most of my time in Quincy. Hopefully they only have me going to TD Garden this Saturday and only this Saturday because I usually have school on Saturday. I have to be at work from 8:00 a.m to 2:00 p.m., but I have class at 9:25 p.m. They say this is only for training, so let's hope the hiring manager was honest about that. She did say there will be a game after that shift, so I might be staying for that too.

CHAPTER 12

Possibilities

It is said that prayer is the best revenge, but that does not mean if you pray for someone to hurt themselves it will happen. Just pray that whatever needs to be done will get done or you get where you want to be in life. Doing that will make people ask, How did he do that? Just be realistic; anything you are able to get you should be able to achieve with prayer, work, and hope. As simple as that.

I was talking to one of my friends about this book last night, and I said, "Basically writing a playbook," but I thought about that comment and figured this is more of a way to write a playbook or how to write it. Like I said before, this should give you the mindset to carry through whatever you encounter.

So I was talking to my friend Fitzy and found out that SpongeBob was originally for adults after he watched a documentary. That makes so much sense now because I interpret the jokes completely differently now versus when I was a child. When I say that, I mean I see the jokes as sexual jokes now; but when I was a kid, they were just innocent and funny. I found that hilarious because it all came together.

Whenever I have to get something done, I imagine the most obscure thing happening. I do that because the most obscure things happen to me, like getting banned from college, not suspended from school but banned from college for something I didn't even get to see. That does not mean I do not do it; that just means I get whatever needs to be done, done as carefully as possible. I have been getting things done doing it that way, and I hope to God nothing changes. Take your time and get your steps figured out before you do them as you get older because your mistakes start having worse outcomes; you can't have that. When I was younger, I just did things at that instance, and that just somehow worked out for me. Now when I say that, I mean whenever you have something imperative for you to figure out what you are doing before, how you get there, what you do while you are there, and what you do after it's done.

The Main Difference

Okay, let me tell you the difference between a girl and a woman. Girls will sit back and look at you a certain way and not tell you what you are doing wrong. Women will actually put effort into finding out why you are like that or doing that and might have a good-ass reason too. You should just know from experience. People are leaving out the fact that I had a traumatic brain injury in this whole equation, not people but girls specifically. I say girls because that is mainly what I am around. I'll catch a woman every once in a while but will somehow mess that up. I need someone to write me a playbook for women just like I'm doing for life, 'cause people tell me I used to know how this goes, but that all went out the window. I really hope this is not what I have to look forward to because this will have my mind twisted.

One thing that I will keep in mind ever since I heard it is "It is just a speed bump, not a brick wall." I mentioned a speed bump a while back, and that just means tread lightly. Life has caught me whenever

I tried to speed up and took me down a few gears. Anything I have had to deal with, I look at as a humbling experience, which means it keeps me mentally centered. Just stay focused, and trust what you are doing in some aspects.

Having that component in your life really will simplify life, and it does that by avoiding endangering situations. I think I have my work schedule at TD Garden figured out with school and everything. I just have to let my scheduling manager know I am not available Tuesday, Thursday, and Saturday because of school. I rarely work at Lids; I might end up at Lids one day or at some game or event the same night. That will be difficult, but I can do it. It is all I have to look forward to. And believe it or not, I was with my friend earlier and a girl asked what he was bringing and he simply said, "Dick and dope." She just laughed and said, "What else?" I just shook my head 'cause I found it odd; I was confused. I cannot wait until my life reenters that phase. I saw something on TV where it said something like the ones crazy enough to change the world are the only ones who do, and I may have that mindset because I want to give a new aspect of life to anyone who reads this. I plan to have a good amount of people read this, and I might change the world.

If you think about it, hope is prayer, because I don't pray as much as some people but I pray, and having hope makes it that much more likely. So whenever I say hope and pray, you can honestly do either or both. Just give the man the time he deserves. Show him his existence. I say this because it has been working for me, and as long as you do your deeds when you can and show him that you know he is there, God is there. Even if you don't get it, it just may not have been meant for you. That's how I look at life anyway; whatever I don't get was not meant for me. It makes things easier to get over with.

Something else I will say is that my mom and stepdad are now strong believers in accidents, because when I was just playing with my sister by the stairs and flipped her around, my mom said she could have done a move and slipped out of my hand. Now that does happen, but she was trying to compare that incident to my incident. The only difference is the man behind it, and I feel that man has more sense, so that accident may be unlikely.

They Don't Know Me

People think they know me after I moved, and I find that kinda funny because no one has seen me enough to say that. At my old house I can admit that I would tend to take less and make that do what it did. But I believe my standards have gone up. I work for what I want and accept nothing less than what I deserve if I can control it. I bring that up because my friend just tried to convince me to take 4.5 for 40 on some dumb shit, and I turned to my friend who hit up another associate who did 6.5 for 40---exactly what I deserved for my budget, even more.

I will be in a podcast with a friend who coincidentally moved from Georgia to Massachusetts when he was younger, and we just happened to play Little League Football together and high school football, and now I will be in his podcast. I don't really know, but I believe that it is a plan being set up, but let me not get too far ahead of myself. I just have high hopes for this whole thing, maybe for things like this book and this podcast, but the book is my main idea, I want to go far..

So this man Jahvae would like to be introduced on a negative note, and he said some shit like, "N be movin' like bitches sometimes I'm fucking" in a song that has other lyrics containing me. Like yo, that is exactly what I'm talking about. No I did not fuck or do anything with him. I sent him a picture the day I woke up because I really did not know if I was gay. He told me, and I was somewhat forced to believe him, but then again, he was going up against a girl who said she loved me. I even tried to see myself taking dick, but I couldn't. I honestly just wanted to see how big his dick was. Not that it is a bad thing; I mean, by all means, do as you please. Just try to be reasonable, and shit happens under certain circumstances---especially any circumstances like mine.

I find it funny how everyone adores you when you are in distress but a few months, maybe a year, after, people forget. And I don't know, but everyone loved me too much, I guess. I got much-needed attention, and that was good, so who am I to complain really? I feel like all the prayers or hopes I received to make it through that coma, got me through that coma. I am so thankful for that. I know I love my life so dearly for a reason. I think there may be a big reason, and I cannot wait to reach it. I feel I'll be a Kijuan who knows his worth and will have a much more meaningful worth. I say that because I know my worth now, but I also know I will be adding meaning to that worth.

The only reason I sent that picture was because I honestly did not know if I was gay or straight because I really did not know what I was doing beforehand. Like I could have sworn I was not doing anything to end up in a coma; it still took a minute to find that out too. I don't remember it, but everyone around me remembers it like it was last week. Well, that's based on stories that I've heard. I know of no one who looks down on me for that, but I feel like everyone thinks I am a weirdo. They can do that 'cause when I'm out, I'm out. No one should be concerned about something I did coming out of a two month coma at eighteen.

And I don't know how to feel about college because I got banned for something that was not mine truthfully, but I'm gonna get what I can get and end it. There is nothing else I can do. I'll just focus on this book, or hopefully I get into UMass Boston and I get my bachelors. That would be a nice ending, if this ends there. Another reason I think this is set up is because when I had the opportunity to dorm, my mom was not trying to hear that option. But as soon as I lost that option, it was, "You can stay at your nana's house." I mean, I respect it because I have that option, but I'm pretty sure if I had that dorm, absolutely nothing I'm dealing with, with college would be happening.

CHAPTER 13

Still Comprehending

I still do not know if I woke from that coma making bad decisions once I hopped in that relationship because of what I did, but it did teach me what not to do. I do not believe it should have been as bad as it has been, but that is partially my fault---from decisions I've made based on the things I was told. People just need to understand this was not a simple bump or bruise but very complex when you think about it. It affected my brain, which stored literally everything except stomach and heart, and that included past memory and maybe a foggy recent memory. I forgot a lot that had to do with relationships; no one tried to teach me. I am learning by myself through trial and error and won't be done with that for a while. I can say I have learned what I needed in the relationship aspect but won't be done with life until it is done. You don't even have to understand it because it might be hard for you; just acknowledge it.

Life comes with mistakes. I think I knew that, and everyone else should know that. Mistakes that people find inexcusable were made, but I think you could see some reasoning behind my mistake. I feel absolutely no one understands one in particular because it is not something you just do. It was just something I did in the hospital out of curiosity---to see how I felt about it and to see an idea of what I play against. And let me tell you, nothing extravagant at all. It actually gave me more belief in myself and just told me I could do it. I felt stronger in a way, and I hadn't seen a gym for two or three months.

My friends and family together are supposed to be my heart and my ears; I say this because Michael Jordan thinks the same exact way. My family has my heart down, but I don't believe my friends are telling me some things for whatever reason, and that is scary. It makes me think something is about to happen. After confronting my friends to get some sort of explanation, they just said, "We love you." But what does that mean? But I'm in my grind period right now, and it has gone smoothly. I have been getting hours at TD and staying afloat in school, but I see more of my friends because I'm not home. I get the look that people wanna tell me something but don't. That pisses me off because when I ask, everyone says, "Oh, I don't know" like that is really what they wanna do, but they carry on to say how much they care about me or how they're so happy I'm here. But I don't believe they care because they would correct my faults if they did. I don't believe I have to force it out because if it doesn't come out, it isn't meant to come out. This is around the time I start to feel like this, but the weather is about to break, and that is usually my time to glow one way or the other.

Friends' Friends

Those aren't my close friends. I should say associates because they only talk to me when they see me, but that carries me on to my close friends: Dyreke, Jeff, Jahvae, Fitzy, Eric, and Sammy. They all think they are slick; I'm not gonna lie to you. But they have never told me anything they didn't make happen, and my friend Will---who is also the former mayor's son---his mom did some things for me too, because I believe she sees what I have in me to do the things we both want happening. He will be doing the editing on this book, so he'll be the first to see the final edition. I chose him to do the editing because I just know he does this. This man played ball at Amherst College, not UMass Amherst but Amherst, and went to Saint Sebastian's for high school. I don't know if they were elite over there, but he was pretty nice from what I saw. Three-pointers were nothing to him, probably still aren't.

One person I have yet to mention is my mentor, my brother, Jamal. He is a very wise young man who gave me a way to look at whatever I dealt with in my life; he told me, "If God told you whatever you had to do to get there, would you do it?" And that made a lot of sense to me because if God gave me a list of what I had to do when I got back down here, I don't believe I would have done it, but maybe I had that in mind.

I bring this up because I was reading *Letters to a Young Brother* by Hill Harper, and that book just made me begin to think about him. I can't just go up the street and see him considering he lives in Georgia and I'm in Massachusetts, but whenever I go down there, we are sure to spend some time together. Whenever I am with him, I feel like I am learning a life lesson. I also consider someone else a brother, whom I met in third grade. He goes by a couple names, but I call him Aj.

He has a whole life now. He got into some legal trouble, not gonna get into that, but has a whole child. Keep in mind, I met him in third grade and he has been to jail and now has a baby. He feels like he doesn't have anyone, and I wish he lived up here with me. He would just have to be down to find a good-paying job and not mind public transportation, just because I'm not driving---I think he knows that.

I think we both have a few things in common, but one thing in particular is the fact that we were both raised by single parents, and I think that played a role in some decisions he has made. But we both had Jamal in our life when I was in Georgia, so the absence of Jamal from his life probably did hurt him. I feel that way after he said, "I don't have anyone," because that means literally no one is helping him. If I get up, we'll make some things happen. Having no biological father in my life really hasn't seemed to affect me, unless I didn't realize or don't remember, but it's life. I came out of the womb with something to put in a book. Look at it either way you want to look at it, but I haven't needed him, so I'm not concerned.

One person I forgot to mention in my close friends list was my main man Josh. I really do not know how I forgot about him, but I did mention him before because he is my friend in the military. I really feel bad for what I just realized, but I apologize, brother. I call him brother because I feel it is important to me to see that he makes it back home in good health, as important as a brother in my case. He will be home soon hopefully, and we have some things planned, so we will discuss what happened there then.

Different Beginnings

I believe the TD Garden job has started to serve its purpose for connections, but it also could have been the only connection I can make, hopefully not. Yesterday I met a professor at UMass Boston who teaches creative writing and also works at TD Garden. He asked me to go give a speech to his class to speak about my accident and the book. That should be easy for me because I spoke a lot about my accident with my therapist and that didn't seem to affect me. The catch is, his class is for fifty and above; that doesn't mean anything to me but more connections.

I was never too specific on who I called my friends. In grade school, if we went to the same school or even went to school in the same town and I knew you, you were a friend. That changed, and I feel it is about that time for things like that to start changing. I just asked myself what I really wanted in a friend. My three top things were loyalty, honesty, and dedication. Loyalty because I do not need to have to think about you turning on me or doing something to hurt me behind my back. Honesty because I need to be able to trust you; if you don't know, just say that. Dedication because I feel it is imperative that I am just as important to you as you are to me.

I feel like I have the mindset of someone in their thirties--- mainly because I am writing a book and I do not know of anyone in my age bracket writing a book. It will become more popular soon, but I want mine to be the first of anyone I know. If this is the first book of anyone I know, then it must be big. That is how I do things. That is how I always did things. I remember me saying something about big things because that is how I do things--- like before all this, which is funny to me because I do not think I remember anything else and I haven't remembered things people told me about and tried to remember. Another reason is because I don't go out much; it's not like I try to all the time. I don't really want to; I don't have the energy to do something required of me to do that.

Last thing I will say is that if I am saying something you disagree with, that is something to talk about. Don't just look at me like why or how; we'd make absolutely no progression, and that is something I like to do. You may no; just say that. Those are two pretty big reasons to me because they come up a lot in my day-to-day life. And if I have ever hurt you and you just never said anything after my hospital visit, I am sorry. I just was not in a proper state of mind; I thought carelessly.

I just put something else together that I think should have been obvious, but my nickname in high school was J_hova, the under score was from me having that name on instagram and I plan to do a movie regarding that. That is life repeating itself in the most positive way that is possible for me. When I realized that I got the warmest feeling in my chest and stomach area, then I just smiled because that really means shit is about to boom soon because these thoughts are just coming to me.

It's about the journey, not the destination, and this has been an interesting journey. I learned a lot and am still learning about myself and life. For example, I learned that I am a strong-minded individual, and that is with my traumatic brain injury. That is due to me having a strong spirit. Learning as far as life goes is basically like last night when I was told I didn't have to pay all the money my first option for a publisher was asking for. So I did my research and found a publisher with their history in hand, and one is about to give me a discount just because of the time I called. That must mean it was meant for me to call because like I said, everything has a reason. My hope is coming back. 2020 may be opening some big doors to some nice places, maybe even some nice cars even though I want to keep my Jetta; it has kept me safe.

It has been a few months, and I have yet to publish this book, and that is simply due to me waiting to hear back from literary agents. I'm waiting so long to be denied, but this will fail a few times before it hits--- the books I am writing especially. My life is day to night, and right now I am in the evening. What do I mean by that? Everything is calm, and I am getting what I want done. That is happening in the midst of me dealing with my sexual dilemma. I don't think I had a choice but to get used to it or the drought, and I chose to get acclimated because that was the wisest decision for me as a person. I think I came up with something, but I gotta focus on the things at hand until then.

G Herbo in his bag and its fur meaning he is doing well, I know that because the music or freestyles have been nothing short of great. I just saw him freestyling on Hot 97, and it goes to show me that life has phases. This includes the fact that Herbo just released an album that goes crazy too, might I add. The PTSD did something to me--- Probably because that was the name of the album, but it was the name of a song by Chance The Rapper too; that song does go hard along with party in heaven and by any means. There is another song I like with lyrics "By any means" but I forgot what it's called. I just remember him singing "By any means" in the chorus. Also if you have any further questions about this book, if I were you I'd follow me on Twitter with my @ on the front page to DM or see another way of how I view things. If you like the little peek of the belt on the back of the book follow my man Edinson @efernandez1211 to get yourself one or any other of his *eccentric* designs.

Lightning Source UK Ltd.
Milton Keynes UK
UKHW042003171220
375465UK00008B/391/J